LIVE LIKE ROYALTY

*Claim Your Inheritance
in the Kingdom of
God and Walk in
Your Divine Purpose*

JAIDA CAMPBELL

LIVE LIKE ROYALTY

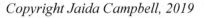

For Greek meanings and clarifications:
https://biblehub.com/greek/

Online article for 4 meanings of love in the Greek:
https://www.thoughtco.com/types-of-love-in-the-bible-700177

Credits for images used in this book:
www.uihere.com/free-cliparts
www.canstockphoto.com

ISBN: 978-1-7330971-0-9

Cover Design by: Heidi Sutherlin

ACKNOWLEDGEMENTS

I want to thank my husband Mike who has encouraged me to follow my dreams and pursue what God has for me. He has been patient when I stayed up late to work on the book. He put up with my crankiness when I had not gotten enough sleep, and he put some boundaries up when I was obsessing. He has been my sounding board when I needed clarification on a biblical question or to shed some light on what I was trying to convey. He is the love of my life, and I would not want to be doing this life without him. He has taken me around the world. He is a wonderful father to our sons and a grandfather as well. We have gotten to experience life together, and I am all the better for it. He introduced me to Jesus and has been my teacher, friend, and sweetheart all these years.

Illustrations by Kylee Campbell: My granddaughter drew the two sketches you will see in the book. She loves to draw and I am trying to convince her that we could write a book together with her drawings and Jesus' inspiration.

I want to thank my mom, Rita Blanchard, who has always encouraged me to be myself and to not let people or the world's expectations guide who I am.

I could not have done this without SELF-PUBLISHING SCHOOL right there with me every step of the way. I have been working on this book for a few years but I always got to the point of asking myself what I was going to do if I ever finished it. And then, along came Self-Publishing School to walk me through it. They give you all the training you need and a coach to encourage you and to answer any questions you may have.

Thank you, Marcy Pusey, for being my coach and helping me to complete this work of love. You were always encouraging. You directed me and guided me through this process, and I appreciate it.

I want to thank the ladies of TRINITYalgood who encourage and challenge me every day. They are supporters of the ministry, and I know that even though they will read this book and be encouraged by it, it is more about them pushing me to pursue God in every area of my life.

Most of all, I want to thank my Savior Jesus Christ and my Heavenly Father who loved me before I even knew of Him. He came into my life and has been by my side all these years. He has been faithful even when I have not been. Jesus has been a friend and brother.

To my granddaughters, Kylee and June.
May you each see yourself
as a princess in our Lord's eye and
walk like a royal all the days of your life.

TABLE OF CONTENTS

INTRODUCTION

Do you want to do something big for God, but you feel stuck? Do you want to grow in your spiritual walk and find your purpose in this big world? Do you wonder sometimes what you are supposed to be doing with your life? You are important and you are worthy of the life God has in store for you.

In my many years of ministry, I have seen countless women who are not living fulfilled in their spiritual lives, and it all boils down to not knowing who they are in Christ and what their rights and privileges are as a member of the Royal Kingdom of God.

I want to introduce you to the fact that you are a royal. The Bible says in I Peter 2:9 (NIV), *"But you are a chosen people, a royal priesthood, a holy nation, God's special possession, that you may declare the praises of him who called you out of darkness into his wonderful light."*

I grew up a tomboy who wanted to play army and football with my brothers. I was definitely not the princess type as a little girl. I still don't consider myself a real "girlie" girl, and I certainly don't expect to be treated in a way that comes across as a queen bee or anything like that. God even saw fit to bless me with boys instead of girls when He was creating my children. He definitely knew what He was doing by giving me only boys. All the girl drama and stuff would have driven me crazy. But I said all that to say this: We are children in God's eyes. We are His children and since we happen to be female that makes us princesses in the Royal Kingdom of God.

We all have a place in the Kingdom of God, but so many of us don't walk that out in our lives. We allow society and circumstances, friends, and family to influence who we are and what we should be doing. Each of us, young or old, rich or poor, executive or stay-at-home mom, has a unique and specific calling that God has predestined for us and it is up to us to find that special something that we have been designed to do. The Kingdom can only work properly if all parts of the Kingdom are in full working mode. If we are not doing our part, the Kingdom is crippled and not fully functional.

To do our part in the Kingdom of God, we must first embrace who we are. We then must take that and apply it to our lives and walk it out fully. I was recently talking to someone who was experiencing a full-blown crisis in her life, and she said, "But I love God and I know the Word." You can love God and "know" the Word, but that is different from actually engaging the Word for it to actively work in your life. We must be fully persuaded and then engaged in what we have learned in an active manner.

I used to be a middle school math teacher, and one of my practices as a math teacher was to give homework every day except Friday. I received plenty of complaints that as a pastor's wife I shouldn't give homework on Wednesdays because of church, but I am a firm believer that you must practice what you learn. If I taught a new concept, then my students ne-eded to practice that concept for it to be a part of them, for them to be able to execute it the next day. It is the same way with the Word of God. Just because someone "knows" the Word doesn't mean they are practicing or applying it to their lives. If my students did not get enough practice solving Algebraic problems, it did not become familiar enough to work through the ones that were more difficult the next day because they had not mastered the basics.

In this book, I will give you the information you need to actively engage in the Word of God to give you the knowledge and confidence you require to fulfill the destiny you have been dreaming about.

I want to give you some tools to put in your tool belt that will help you to walk in victory and fullness of life as you endeavor to walk out your life of faith. It will not be easy. It will not be a cake walk. Anything worthwhile takes work. If you are skating through life and there is no discomfort or difficulties, then you need to ramp up what you expect of yourself and give God your best. Get out of your comfort zone and make some waves in your comfortable life. If you are having struggles already, then be prepared to take the next step in this walk with God as a member of His Royal Family to fully realize who you are in Christ and the power of that name.

So, get into this book about your position in the Kingdom of God and be amazed at the life that you can live if you truly understand who you are and how to apply the Word of God in your life.

How to get the most out of **Live Like Royalty**:

1. There are several scriptures in each chapter. I encourage you to write the scriptures that you want to apply to your life on index cards and keep them close, maybe tape them to your bathroom mirror and refrigerator, anywhere that you look several times a day. Take every opportunity to read and say out loud the Word of God. The more we say them, the more they become part of our belief system, and the Word will build our spirit up inside of us.

2. Look out for **Reflection** within each chapter. Take the time to think about what you had read to that point so that you can digest the meanings and ideas that I have proposed in these chapters. You can "love God and know the Bible" but unless you have engaged the Word in an active manner, you are not applying it to your life.

3. At the end of each chapter, there are a few questions for **Journal Responses**. Be honest in your answers and let the Word of God transform what you believe about yourself and encourage you to be all that God has for you.

4. As a Small Group Study, you can very easily spend time with friends learning about who you are and discussing the truths introduced in this book. You can encourage each other as you grow in the knowledge of who you are in Christ and how you fit into the kingdom of God. There are a couple of ways that you can do this as a Small Group Study. One way is to have everyone read the chapter in advance and do the **Reflections** within the chapter and answer the **Journal Responses** at the end of the chapter before you meet. Another way would be

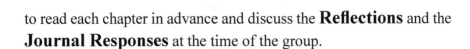

to read each chapter in advance and discuss the **Reflections** and the **Journal Responses** at the time of the group.

Whichever way you choose to the complete this book, you will be blessed and encouraged by it!

Now, let's get to work!

CHAPTER 1

For Such a Time as This

Esther 4:14 (NKJV)

*"Yet who knows whether
you have come to the kingdom
for such a time as this?"*

I was watching the movie "Grace of Monaco" recently and was struck by the concept that Grace Kelly, an American actress who married Prince Rainier to become the Serene Highness Princess Grace of Monaco, had to change her idea of what she believed to be the fairy tale of royalty to the reality of living as royalty. There was a point when she had to put some real work into being what was expected of her in the royal family.

I Peter 2:9 (NIV) says,

"But you are a chosen people, a royal priesthood, a holy nation, God's special possession, that you may declare the praises of him who called you out of darkness into his wonderful light."

If you are a believer, a follower of Jesus Christ, you have a responsibility to walk in His wonderful light so that others may see as well. And walking in that means you must understand who you are in the family. Webster's Dictionary says that "royal" as an adjective means "having the status of a king or queen or a member of their family" or, as a noun, "a member of a royal family." You are a member of the royal family of the Kingdom of God.

It—of course—is not run like any other kingdom and the royals of this family are not like any other royals but we can learn from what we know of earthly royals and their families. But just as Princess Grace learned in her role, there is work to be done to do our part and to live the life of a royal. God expects us to take our place, but we cannot fully do that if we do not first understand who we are, what our rights are, and how we can walk that out.

With that status of being a "royal" and having the benefits and rights of the royal family, there is some work to be done to live up what is expected of us as children of the Living God. I am not talking about what is expected by people or the world, but what is expected by our Heavenly Father and to live up to the honor He has bestowed on us when He gave His best, His Son, Jesus Christ, to take our place on the cross for our sins.

I grew up in a mainstream church that did not teach salvation, or "getting saved and becoming a believer." And because I did not spend any time really learning about Jesus and the details of what His presence on this earth meant and ultimately His death and resurrection, I was clueless that I was on my way to a life of destruction.

When I got engaged to be married, I decided that I needed to "settle down" to become a dutiful wife and, my idea of settling down was to attend church once a week for appearances. My fiancé introduced me to another kind of church that met on Wednesdays. I'd never heard of that before, church on Wednesdays? I was curious. After two Wednesdays in a row, we found ourselves in a "cell group." This was the 80's and it was the beginning of small groups. We met every Friday and had dinner and testimonies.

Not knowing what I was getting myself into, I was excited about meeting new people and making new married friends. In those eight weeks, my life was transformed. I heard 16 testimonies of how people's lives were changed after receiving Jesus as their Savior. I had never heard of such a thing, and I was fascinated. Needless to say, by the time that last week was finished, I had prayed my own prayer of salvation.

Not only did I meet Jesus as my Savior, I became a member of this Royal Family of God and met fellow believers who would be encouragers in my life as I learned more about my Heavenly Father and my Savior Jesus Christ. I also had a lot to learn about what it means to be a believer. I was 20 years old and felt like my life had only just begun. I soaked up everything I could about my new life, and understanding my position, my rights, my responsibilities, and my benefits were just the beginning. My prayer is that you will gain more knowledge and understanding concerning these things as you continue to grow in your walk with the Lord.

There is a royal in the Old Testament that is similar to Serene Highness Princess Grace of Monaco in that she was not born into royalty and therefore did not expect to live the life of a royal. Let's look into Esther's story and what she can teach us about becoming royalty and walking in the light of it.

In the Book of Esther, I won't go into all the political climate of the times or why the king acted as he did toward his wife Queen Vashti. What I want to focus on is God's plan to put a young woman in a place of influence years before she or anyone else knew that that influence would save not only her life, but the lives of a nation of people.

When the king demanded that his Queen Vashti show herself so that he could boast about her beauty to his guests, she was offended and refused to come. In that day, this would have been an inappropriate request on the king's part, and when she refused to come, he was embarrassed and became furious. It did not help that his advisors told him that if he did not do something about her "attitude," this attitude would permeate the kingdom and all the women would then refuse to do what was expected of them. He listened to his advisors and readily agreed that Queen Vashti must be put away so that she would not have any influence on the women of the kingdom.

We already see that the king could be easily influenced by his advisors, and you will see this again later in the story concerning the Jews. He was also persuaded to find another woman to take the place of Queen Vashti. This is where Esther comes into the picture.

Beautiful virgins from all over the kingdom were brought to the palace and treated well, fed, clothed, and pampered to make them presentable to the king for his inspection. Esther was caught up in the net of beautiful virgins, and in her meekness, humility, and beauty, she stood out—not only to the head eunuch, but also to the king who chose Esther to be his queen.

I am sure that she was not sure what had happened to her and why. She had been taken from her home that she was raised in, the home of her cousin Mordecai, who took her in when her parents died. She was Jewish but Mordecai had advised her to hide her ethnicity and religion. She was cut off from her family and her culture. She was at the mercy of the king who did not understand her or who she was.

When a plan of total annihilation of the Jewish race was created by a favored adviser of the king, Mordecai sent a message to Esther that she must do something. She was the only one in a position to make a difference. In Esther 4, when Esther asked Mordecai what was going on, Mordecai sent back to her through her messenger the plan on how the Jews were to be destroyed. At first, Esther said that she did not think that she could do anything and that she could die if she tried. But when Mordecai admonishes her,

"Do not think in your heart that you will escape in the king's palace any more than all the other Jews. 14 For if you remain completely silent at this time, relief and deliverance will arise for the Jews from another place, but you and your father's house will perish. Yet who knows whether you have come to the kingdom for such a time as this?" (Esther 4:14).

Mordecai believed that Esther had been put in the palace to influence the king in some way to save the Jewish people. This was not seen beforehand that we know of from the scriptures, but it looked as if God had it worked out in advance to have Esther in the palace as the queen so that she could do something to stop this plan against the Hebrew people.

I always tell people who come to me with their concerns, such as the loss of a job or marriage trouble, that God was not surprised by this. He has been working on their behalf before they even knew of the problem.

Rest in the Almighty God who knows things in advance and sets things in place for rescue, restoration, and deliverance. Esther did not know that she had been placed in a special position of influence at the time, and she needed to be persuaded that her time had come to do her part. It is very common for most of us to have those moments of insecurity about stepping out to be who God has called us to be.

Has there been a time when you felt the same as Esther, hesitant in thinking that you are worthy or able to what you were asked to do?

_____

_____

_____

_____

_____

The funny thing about the fact that I'm writing a book that has anything to do with princesses is that I was a total tomboy as a kid. I had two brothers, one older and one younger, and I wanted to do everything they did. Football, army, building forts.

Check this picture out.

Don't I look excited about having a "princess party" for my 5th birthday? My mom said that by the end of the party I had made everyone miserable. I never did like playing with dolls so the Barbie doll, baby doll, or princess concept were not at all interesting when I would rather be outside playing army and football with my brothers and the other kids in the neighborhood. My parents gave me a doll every Christmas, thinking that I would come around one day; instead, I would cry because my brothers got really cool stuff like machine guns and guitars.

You could say that I was a reluctant princess. But now as an adult and understanding my place in the Kingdom of God, I want to do all that He has called me to do. And I feel compelled to share this message of empowerment with others.

I Peter 2:9 (NIV) says,

"But you are a chosen people, a royal priesthood, a holy nation, God's special possession, that you may declare the praises of him who called you out of darkness into his wonderful light."

Let's look at this scripture again. It says that we are "a chosen people." This tells me that it was not by accident or happenstance. God chose us and He chose each of us for a reason. There is something each of us is supposed to do and He has us on this earth to do it.

Let's make this perfectly clear: God did choose us but that does not mean he did not choose others. It means God chose mankind, and He chose each person for a specific purpose. He chose you to be you. He created you to be the way you are as part of His chosen people.

Do you feel like you are part of a "chosen people?"

_____

_____

_____

_____

_____

I also like the phrase "God's special possession" in the above scripture. Have you ever had any special possessions? When we were children, we would take those special possessions and put them in some kind of treasure box or hidden place that protected these treasures from harm or theft. We had marbles, tokens of special memories, smooth rocks, a piece of jewelry. These were special possessions and we wanted to keep them safe.

As adults, we have special possessions as well. I have some antiques of my parents that are special to me. I now own the antique oak table around which my family gathered to have meals for as long as I can remember. That is a special possession of mine. I take very good care of it. We all take extreme care of the treasures that we deem special. It is the same with God. He deems us special possessions and He takes care of us in that manner.

But let's look at the last part of that scripture. It says, "…that you may declare the praises of him who called you out of darkness into his wonderful light." This gives us a statement of why He has chosen us; why we are a royal priesthood, a holy nation, God's special possession. We are to declare! Synonyms for "declare" are proclaim, announce, reveal, broadcast.

So, we are to broadcast, announce, and proclaim the praises of the One who has called us out of darkness. We were in darkness and He brought us out of that darkness and into His wonderful light. I think of the times that I've been in a dark place like a tunnel or a cave, and it might not even be a bad experience. It might have been a hike or driving through a tunnel, but when I get back out into the light, there is a relief, a lifting of the spirit that comes at that moment.

Picture a time when you have been in a dark place and then you are out into the light—that fresh and bright moment of illumination. God gives us that when we receive Jesus as our Savior. He brings us out of darkness and brings us into His marvelous light. It is a whole new world of light and brightness. And we are to proclaim His praises. As an influencer in the Kingdom of God, we must be vocal in our praises of Him and to spread the light that He has given us.

Can you think of ways in which we can be vocal about our praises?

_____

_____

_____

_____

_____

You are in your place of influence because God has put you there. You are the influencer in your world, whether that is in the office, in the school, as an at-home mom, with your family, in the gym. You have been moved into your position for such a time as this. Just as Grace Kelly had to work at being what was expected of her as a royal, you must put the work into being who God wants you to be for His Kingdom.

You are a daughter of the Living God with all the rights and benefits of that position. We are going to talk more about those rights and benefits in the coming chapters. You will learn to put those rights and benefits to work for you and you will be equipped to fulfill the plan and purpose that God has for you. You will also learn to influence the ones around you for God and His Kingdom. Let people know who you are and whose you are. For such a time as this, let people know what He has done in your life and be the light that others are craving.

1. How does the story of Esther resonate with you? Do you identify with her or do you see yourself differently?

_____

_____

_____

_____

_____

2. Has there been a time when you felt God had a specific thing for you to do? Did you feel the confidence to act on it?

_____

_____

_____

_____

_____

3. Do you sometimes feel out of place or not bold enough to influence others? What can help you to have the boldness that it takes to share your life and be an influencer?

_____

_____

_____

_____

_____

4. What scripture from this chapter will you focus on this week and why?

_____

_____

_____

_____

_____

If you have never asked Jesus to become your Savior and you want to receive Him and begin to walk in the fullness of your life in Jesus, you may say the following prayer out loud and join the Royal Family of God.

Heavenly Father,
Thank you for sending Jesus to this earth to become the spotless Lamb to take my place on the cross for my sins and sickness, for my iniquities and shortcomings. I confess that I am a sinner and I ask you right now to come into my heart, come into my life.

Help me to overcome temptation of my old life and give me the ability and strength to follow you all the days of my life. I receive you now, Jesus, into my heart to make you my Savior and the Lord of my life.

In Jesus' name,
Amen.

You have just received Jesus into your heart as your Lord and Savior. Yes, it is that simple. The rest of the book will help you to understand what you just did and to give you the knowledge and understanding to help you live a life of victory and fulfillment.

CHAPTER 2

The Position of a Princess

Romans 8:15-17 (NKJV)

*"For you did not receive the spirit of bondage again to fear,
but you received the Spirit of adoption by whom we cry out,
"Abba, Father."
16 The Spirit Himself bears witness with our spirit that we are
children of God, 17 and if children, then heirs—heirs of God and
joint heirs with Christ, if indeed we suffer with Him,
that we may also be glorified together."*

When I think of a princess, of course, I think of the pomp and circumstance of it all, the beauty and grace with which she must walk through life. Oh, I can imagine the mornings waking up to the beauty of the palace bedroom with all its luxury. I can see in my mind's eye the opulence of the furniture and fixtures. I can see myself being waited on by my lady's maid, getting my bath ready, pressing my clothes, getting my make up on, and having my hair done so that I don't have bad hair days ever again. Then I see myself going over my itinerary for the day and having my driver pick me up to take me to my first very important appointment... Oh, sorry, I got a little carried away with my daydreaming of being a princess.

But besides all the luxury and pampering, there are also the practical matters of royal life and the central part of that is her position in the royal family. As a princess, she is in direct lineage after her mother and father. She does not wonder if she is accepted as the princess or question her right to be in the family. She does not wake up and wonder if she has been good enough to be a part of the royal family. She knows that she is born into this family and her position in the family is as solid as a rock.

Has anyone ever treated you like a princess? How did that make you feel?

_____

_____

_____

_____

Let's think about how that correlates with the Kingdom of God. Once you have asked Jesus Christ to become your Savior, you are immediately part of this Royal Family, the Royal Family of God. In John 3:3 (NKJV)

"Jesus answered and said to him,
'Most assuredly, I say to you, unless one is born again,
he cannot see the kingdom of God.'"

So, looking at the opposite of this, that would mean that being born again, you will see the Kingdom of God. When we are born again, we are born into the KINGDOM OF GOD—the Royal Family of God. It then says in John 3:5 (NKJV)

"Jesus answered, 'Most assuredly, I say to you, unless one is born of water and the Spirit, he cannot enter the kingdom of God. 6 That which is born of the flesh is flesh, and that which is born of the Spirit is spirit.'"

When we receive Jesus as our Savior, we are born of the Spirit. We are now talking about the spirit realm. We still have our natural parents and our natural siblings, but this puts us in the family of God, in line with our Heavenly Father, our spiritual Father. We are in direct lineage with our Heavenly Father.

According to Romans 8:12 in the NIV, once we are reborn into the Kingdom of God, we have an obligation to live by the spirit.

"Therefore, brothers and sisters,
we have an obligation—but it is not to the flesh,
to live according to it."

Then verses 13 and 14 says,

"For if you live according to the flesh, you will die;
but if by the Spirit you put to death the misdeeds of the body,
you will live."

We are commanded or obligated to live by the spirit and the way to do that is to understand that we are in the family of God and this gives us certain rights and benefits as the children of God.

How do you feel about the word "obligation" in the Romans 8:12-14?

_____

_____

_____

_____

_____

In Romans 8:16-17 in the NKJV,

> *"The Spirit Himself bears witness with our spirit that we are children of God, and if children, then heirs—heirs of God and joint heirs with Christ, if indeed we suffer with Him, that we may also be glorified to-gether."*

Because we are born again and children of the Living God, we are heirs of Him and joint heirs with Christ. So, God is our Heavenly Father and Jesus is our Heavenly brother. Jesus is a brother who is willing to share his inheritance with us and there is plenty to go around.

As Americans, we don't truly grasp the idea of inheritance other than money and property. But when you are dealing with royalty and lineage, there are other things that are inherited, such as the title, the name, the heritage, the reputation, along with the land and property of the family.

There is a certain pecking order in all the families regarding who inherits what and so forth. Position in the family is very important. So, when we are talking about being an heir of God and joint heir with Christ, this encompasses everything that that entails, including your position in the Kingdom. No one can take away your position in this Royal Family of the Kingdom of God.

No one can separate us from God's inheritance. But we must first accept that we can stand in our position in the Royal Family of God boldly and rightfully so. And because this is a spiritual family, God has done something that cannot happen in a natural family. We are all treated as if we are the firstborn. So, we inherit the position of the firstborn just as Jesus is His only begotten Son and yet we inherit everything along with Jesus.

What does it mean to you to be an heir?

_____

_____

_____

_____

_____

I used to work in the Trust Department of a bank in a small town in Mississippi. The Trust Department is where estates and trusts are established and handled for families. If a customer dies, they may have put in their will that certain monies are put in a trust for family members. Or even before someone passes away, a person can set up a trust for one or more people. It stipulates how much money there is and how it is going to be handled and distributed. I certainly won't go into all of that, but let's just say that money sometimes brings the worst out of people.

When we are talking about heirs and joint-heirs, we are speaking of people who inherit the property of the person who has passed away. Sometimes the will is read and everyone is okay with how it all worked out, but there are times when people are not happy about their share or how it is going to be handled. I have seen people act extremely ugly over what was being inherited and to whom it was going. Some people fight over amounts of money or certain personal items. Some squabble over who is going to run the business or why an extra person has been written into the will. Let's just say that money is the ultimate separator of families.

But in the Kingdom of God, we all inherit everything. And Jesus chose to die on the cross to give us the right to inherit it all when He could have had it all to himself. He was our Father's only begotten Son. But when He took our place on the cross, poured His blood on the mercy seat, rose again, and ascended into heaven, He allowed us to become sons and daughters of the Most High along with Him, and not only that, but God set it up so that we all share in the inheritance equally. So, Jesus chose to die on the cross and also chose to share His inheritance equally. Let's stop and think about what that really means.

As I said earlier, we don't always understand all that we inherit because it is more than money. It is the title, the name, the heritage, the reputation, and the land and property of the family.

We can go all the way back to the Book of Genesis to the beginning, to establish something that a lot of women have difficulty believing about themselves.

Gen 1:1-31 in the Message Bible, it says,

> *"God looked over everything he had made;*
> *it was so good, so very good!"*

Let's make this very clear: God don't make no junk. (Excuse the grammar for effect!) Every time God created something, He declared it to be good. That includes His most precious creation, man and woman. If you cannot think good of yourself, then you are not comprehending the position you have yourself in right now as a child of God. You have inherited the title and the reputation of the Kingdom of God. Your position is secure in the family.

You can always make the argument that man had fallen and now we are not perfect anymore, but don't forget these words in Romans...

Romans 5:18-19 (NIV), "Consequently, just as one trespass resulted in condemnation for all people, so also one righteous act resulted in justification and life for all people. For just as through the disobedience of the one man the many were made sinners, so also through the obedience of the one man the many will be made righteous."

So yes, through Adam we lost our place in the Kingdom, but through Jesus's sacrifice of taking our place as the sacrificial lamb, we are now back in fellowship and righteousness with our Heavenly Father. Righteousness means right standing. So, we are in "right standing" with our Father if we have repented and asked Jesus to be our Savior.

When we are in "right standing" with our Father, we are confident to walk up to Him and spend time with Him with no qualms about our right to be there. This gives you the right to take your position in the Royal Family of God. You have the spirit inside of you and He wants to see you walking in the position that has been made for you and waiting for you to fill.

Have you ever had an argument or misunderstanding with a friend or family member? Or maybe you have done something to offend or hurt someone? How do you feel when you are in that person's presence? Do you feel confident in your relationship with that person, or is your conversation with him/her stilted or uncomfortable? That's what happens when we are not in perfect relationship with someone. Would you feel comfortable asking that person for a favor while you are in this point of your relationship? I would say probably not.

But that is not how our relationship with God is. This is where understanding your position in the Kingdom of the God is so important. We must

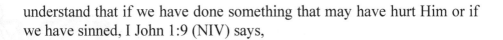

understand that if we have done something that may have hurt Him or if we have sinned, I John 1:9 (NIV) says,

"If we confess our sins, He is faithful and just to forgive us our sins and to cleanse us from all unrighteousness."

It says, "He is faithful and just to forgive us and cleanse us." Once we are forgiven and cleansed, our relationship with God is restored and we are now able to spend time with Him AS IF NOTHING HAPPENED. I can look back as a child and remember that I was always welcome in my father's lap whenever I approached him. He did not turn me away after I had messed up and done something wrong. He welcomed me with open arms. He loved me and wanted me to sit in his lap. It is the same with our Heavenly Father.

Keep in mind that He created a plan to send His only begotten Son, to take our place on the cross so that He can have fellowship with us. He made the ultimate sacrifice for you and me to spend time with Him. It would have defeated His purpose if, after all He did for His creation, He would then turn us away when we needed Him the most. Everything He did was for that—to be able to spend time with us. He has made a way for us to boldly walk up to Him and sit on His lap, once again in 1 John 1:9.

Think about 1 John 1:9 and what it means to you.

_____

_____

_____

_____

_____

So, you see that no matter what we do, He has made a way for us to be in "right standing" with Him so that He can have fellowship with His children. Isaiah 43:25 (NKJV) says plainly,

> *"I, even I, am He who blots out your transgressions*
> *for My own sake; And I will not remember your sins."*

It does not say He will forget as if He could be absent-minded. He says, "I will not remember your sins." This is a choice He makes every time we repent. He chooses to not remember our sins once we ask for forgiveness. When we know that He forgives us and chooses to not remember what we have done, we can walk into His presence with our heads held high for we are confident that He loves us and does not see the wrongs we had done. But also notice in that same scripture He said, "for My own sake." He blots out MY transgressions for HIS sake. He chooses to forget MY sins against HIM for HIS sake. Wow, He does it to benefit Him! And what benefit is that? So that He can have fellowship with us. So that our position in the family is still clear and stable.

Once again, we are back to why He created us, why He sent His Son to take our place on the cross, and why He put in I John 1:9—all of this so that He can be with us! All of this is so that He can spend time with us! When we don't walk in this knowledge, He is disappointed because He did all of this so that we can be with Him. He is waiting for us to walk in full awareness of our position with Him in this Royal Family of God. Because when we can walk in full awareness of our position, we are walking in confidence of who we are in Christ and who we are in the Royal Family of God.

What benefit does God have to forgive our sins in reference to Isaiah

43:25? What does that mean to you?

_____

_____

_____

_____

_____

Just as the princess of the royal family has a position and she is confident in that position, we can walk in that same confidence. God does not change His mind. He is faithful and trustworthy in His promises. You are a princess of the Royal Family. And with that comes the confidence to walk with your head held high because you are the King's kid. Your position in the Kingdom of God is secure.

1. What evidence do we have that we are part of a royal family? What does that mean to you?

_____

_____

_____

_____

2. Is this concept of being part of a royal family difficult for you to comprehend? Why or why not?

_____

_____

_____

_____

_____

3. Do you have a good example of an earthly father or do you struggle in this area? Do you see God as your Heavenly Father? What does that mean to you?

_____

_____

_____

_____

_____

4. What scripture from this chapter do you believe spoke to you the most and why?

_____

_____

_____

_____

_____

CHAPTER 3

Your Kingdom Benefits

2 Peter 1:2-4 (NIV)

*Grace and peace be multiplied to you in the knowledge
of God and of Jesus our Lord, as His divine power has given to us all
things that pertain to life and godliness, through the knowledge
of Him who called us by glory and virtue,
by which have been given to us exceedingly great and precious promises,
that through these you may be partakers of the divine nature,
having escaped the corruption that is in the world through lust.*

When you are looking for a job, one of the things that you look into is the benefit package that comes with the employment. Some jobs have better benefits than others. Some offer medical, dental, and optical insurance. Some even include retirement, stock options, and such. When you sign up for these benefits, these are promises that they will uphold as long as you are in their employment and stay within the guidelines given. When you sign up for these benefits, do you constantly wonder if they are telling the truth about these promises? Do you question whether they are putting your money into the IRA that you have established with them? You may look at your pay stub every once in a while, as a cautionary measure, which is practical to do, to see that it is coming out of your check. And you should check your account to make sure the money is being deposited. But basically, you believe that these benefits or promises are being kept by your employer.

God has benefits as well when you "sign up" to be a part of His Kingdom. These are the promises that are stated in the Word of God that He has given to all believers. Just like you get a handbook or manual or benefit packet to explain all the benefits available to you on your job, we have our handbook or manual in the Word of God.

The New Living Translation says in 2 Peter 1:2-4:

> *"May God give you more and more grace and peace as you grow*
> *in your knowledge of God and Jesus our Lord.*
> *3 By his divine power, God has given us everything*
> *we need for living a godly life.*
> *We have received all of this by coming to know him,*
> *the one who called us to himself by means*
> *of his marvelous glory and excellence.*
> *And because of his glory and excellence,*
> *he has given us great and precious promises.*
> *These are the promises that enable you to share his divine nature*
> *and escape the world's corruption caused by human desires."*

The Living Bible version says it this way:

"Do you want more and more of God's kindness and peace? Then learn to know him better and better. ³ For as you know him better, he will give you, through his great power, everything you need for living a truly good life: he even shares his own glory and his own goodness with us! ⁴ And by that same mighty power he has given us all the other rich and wonderful blessings he promised; for instance, the promise to save us from the lust and rottenness all around us, and to give us his own character."

Before we look at some of those promises (there are more than we could possibly cover in this chapter) I want you to make note of the second part of Verse 3.

Notice in verse 3…

"His divine power has given us everything."

What? *Everything we need for a godly life.* How? Through our knowledge of Him; by coming to know him. It says that we receive ALL of this by coming to know him. How do we get to know someone? We must spend time with that person. It is the same with our Heavenly Father. We must spend time with Him to come to know Him. God makes it so simple, but we make it so hard. To know Him is to learn of His character, His honesty, His integrity, and then trust comes. You may come from a situation that caused you to lose trust in someone or in mankind, but God is the picture of trustworthiness. You will only know this—really know this—once you have spent time with Him.

It is like once you get to know someone to be trustworthy and honest, then you will trust that person with your money, or with your car, or whatever you deem valuable. If you are not trusting God with your life, with your finances, with protection, with your prosperity, then you don't truly trust Him; therefore, you do not KNOW Him. It's a trust issue.

What do you trust God with? And what do you not trust God with?

_____

_____

_____

_____

_____

The promises of God are just like our benefits of the Kingdom. Let's break down some of the benefits so that we can understand what kind of advantages we have when we begin walking in the promises or benefits of this life.

One of the benefits of the Kingdom is our self-image. People, and specifically women, struggle with their self-image. But our self-image should come from our Father and no one else. It says in Gen 1:27 (NIV),

"So, God created mankind in his own image, in the image of God he created them; male and female he created them."

It can't get any clearer than that: We are created in His image. As children of the Living God, we should not be having image issues, and yet we do. We must believe who He says that we are. I love that Mary the mother of Jesus said to the angel who told of her upcoming child, *"I am the Lord's servant. May everything you have said about me come true."* (NLT)

We must believe what God says about us, that we are created in His image. Conqueror, warrior, overcomer; redeemed, righteous, one who is loved. Trustworthy, selfless, bold, beautiful, all of these and more. It is our choice to walk in the knowledge of Him and who we are in Him.

What are some traits like God that you believe about yourself? Name something that you want to grow in concerning your self-image?

_____

_____

_____

_____

_____

Another benefit of being a member of the Royal Family of God is our inheritance. Romans 8:17 in the NIV says,

"Now if we are children, then we are heirs—heirs of God and co-heirs with Christ, if indeed we share in his sufferings in order that we may also share in his glory."

Think about what it means in the world and how we inherit what has been left behind by our parents or close relatives. But with God, it is more than money and property. All He is, his character and all, are ours if we just know Him and trust Him. But not only are we "heirs of God", we are "joint-heirs with Christ."

What is Christ's is mine. He saw fit to give up glory for a season and come down here to share His inheritance with us. This also covers prosperity. He wants us to be successful just like any father would want his children to be successful in their area of livelihood.

Our three boys are successful in their fields and we are proud parents. Don't you think God is proud of His children when they are successful? Don't you think He would do whatever it takes to make His children successful in life?

Protection is another benefit of the Kingdom of God. Insurance companies offer all kinds of protection, and now they even offer Identity Theft Protection. These insurance companies offer a way to pay for the damage after something happens to us. But Psalm 91(NKJV) is a perfect example of godly protection,

"He who dwells in the secret place of the Most High shall abide under the shadow of the Almighty. I will say of the LORD,
"He is my refuge and my fortress;
My God, in Him I will trust."

I know that I can count on my Heavenly Father to protect me. My earthly father was a big man, and I knew that he would protect me if anything happened to me. I used to say he was the biggest dad on the block. He was tough and he loved me. I was confident of those things and most things did not scare me because I knew I had a dad who would protect me.

I am proud to say that my Heavenly Father is the biggest dad on the block and I know that He is bigger than anything that comes my way. He stations angels around me and my family to keep us protected. He is the shadow that I can hide under and the fortress that I can run to for protection and shielding from the storm.

Where do you stand on the benefits of prosperity and protection? Do you believe God offers prosperity to His children? Do you believe He can protect you?

_____

_____

_____

_____

_____

Your health and the health of your family is another benefit of the Kingdom of God. Isaiah 53:5 (NKJV) in the Old Testament prophesied,

> *"But He was wounded for our transgressions,*
> *He was bruised for our iniquities;*
> *The chastisement for our peace was upon Him,*
> *And by His stripes we are healed."*

He put the plan in place before Jesus was born on this earth that we could walk in divine health and, if we get sick, we can ask and be healed. Most of us think we don't deserve healing or that healings don't happen anymore or that we are too insignificant for Him to bother with our healing.

Remember: It all comes back to trusting Him and who He is. Healing is for the present and God is our Great Physician. My earthly father would want me to be a healthy person; he would want me to be well. It's the same for Our Heavenly Father. He wants His children well. We have already established that we are His children. He wants us healthy, and if He has the ability – which we know He does because He is the Almighty God – He would do whatever it took to make us well.

Isaiah 53 is a prophecy many years before Jesus' birth about the Messiah dying on the cross. And then in 1 Peter 2:24, it refers back to the scripture in Isaiah in which it says,

"who Himself bore our sins in His own body on the tree, that we, having died to sins, might live for righteousness—by whose stripes you were healed."

There are two parts of what Jesus did on the cross for us. As you can see from this scripture in Isaiah 53, our sins are forgiveness but also our sicknesses are healed. The faith that it takes to receive salvation is the same faith we should apply to receive our healing as well.

Being able to walk in peace is another benefit or promise that we have as children of the Most High. John 14:27 (NKJV) says,

"Peace I leave with you, My peace I give to you; not as the world gives do I give to you. Let not your heart be troubled, neither let it be afraid."

We can walk in a peace that the world does not understand. It says "Jesus's peace!" Do you understand what that means? The peace that Jesus walked in the times when His enemies wanted to kill Him. The peace by which He calmed the sea. The peace that helped Him on the way to Golgotha. We have His peace in us because He gave it to us.

My husband and I have three grown boys now and we definitely had our times of concerns, but we continually put our concerns into the Lord's hands. I used this scripture to keep me encouraged during those times when my boys were not doing great. We are told in the world that a mother must worry to be a good mother. We walk around with this badge of honor pinned to our chest that says, "I worry about my children." But the Bible says in Matthew 6:25-34 (NIV),

"Therefore I tell you, do not worry about your life, what you will eat or drink; or about your body, what you will wear. Is not life more than food, and the body more than clothes? Look at the birds of the air; they do not

sow or reap or store away in barns, and yet your heavenly Father feeds them. Are you not much more valuable than they? Can any one of you by worrying add a single hour to your life? ..."

Can we add anything to our lives by worrying? It is a waste of time and energy when we should be praying about the situation. Our Lord takes care of the birds of the air, so how much more would He take care of His own children? If we cannot put the concern into the Lord's hands, then we are not trusting him and we are back to the trust issue.

1 Peter 5:7 (NIV) tells us to:

"Cast all your anxiety on him because he cares for you."

Cast means to throw (something) forcefully in a specific direction. One of the synonyms for cast is pitch. So, this is a purposeful throw, a forceful pitch away from you and to God. We could look at it like a pitcher in a baseball game. He pitches it to the catcher. We don't want to have it thrown back, but my point is it is a purposeful and forceful throw with direction and skill. We are told to cast or throw these anxieties, concerns, and worries to the Lord for He cares for us. Just as a father wants to take on the cares of his child, our Heavenly Father wants to handle it for us. And if we know our Heavenly Father the way we should, we would trust that He will take care of it.

The promise of peace in John 14:27 says that we can walk in the same kind of peace that Jesus walked in when He walked and carried his cross to Golgotha. It says that I can have His peace, not what the world calls peace. And to do that, we must cast these worries to Him, to trust that when we cast the problems to Him, He will take care of it. It may not be in our timing or in the way we would like for it to be handled, but we must believe that He is beside us through the whole situation.

What does it look like to have peace in your life? Are you walking in peace right now or is this something that you need to work toward?

_____

_____

_____

_____

_____

These are just a few of the precious promises that we can walk in if we choose to increase our knowledge of our Heavenly Father. His promises to us are similar to the benefits package we receive with our employment. When we are approached by our Human Resource person, we accept that these benefits are provided for us and that we can count on the policies. It is baffling to me that we have more trust in this than what our mighty God has promised us. But it really does boil down to our knowledge or lack of knowledge of the Word and the promises within it.

Now a few more thoughts concerning 2 Peter 1:2-4; Notice that it has been done BY HIS DIVINE POWER and because of HIS GLORY AND EXCELLENCE. Think about God's power. If these promises are fulfilled by His power, there is nothing that can defeat or extinguish the power that is behind these promises.

It has nothing to with our ability or our worthiness. It has to do with His glory and excellence. We don't deserve these promises nor do we earn them. We inherit them because we are His children. It is part of the big plan when He sent Jesus to take our place on the cross. As much as we want to denounce or ignore what He has done for us, we cannot change the fact that He has already put these promises into place. It is our responsibi-

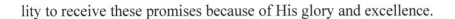

lity to receive these promises because of His glory and excellence.

And He set it up this way so that we can share in His divine nature like a father wants to share his love of baseball with his son or a mother sharing her love of cooking with her children. Another reason is because He wants us to be able to escape the corruption of the world.

We must be able to trust what the Word says about us, about our God, and about the promises that we can apply to our lives. These are precious promises that we have been given freely from our Heavenly Father. Like any father, He wants to share Himself with us and protect us from dangerous elements in the world. If we want these things for our children, how much more does our Heavenly Father want these things for His children?

1. As an employee of a company, each year I am asked to go over my benefits and determine if I want to make changes. Consider the promises of God as benefits. Which one is the easiest to believe and why? Which one is the most difficult to believe and why?

_____

_____

_____

_____

_____

2. Have you ever been asked to take care of something and then that person keeps asking you about it or goes behind your back to see if you did it or not? How does that make you feel? How does that relate to

the promise of peace when it discusses the idea of casting your cares upon Him?

_____

_____

_____

_____

_____

3. Pick one of these promises (benefits) each week at a time and meditate on it. Find the scriptures mentioned in the chapter concerning each one and find at least one more to corroborate it.

_____

_____

_____

_____

_____

4. What scripture from this chapter will you focus on this week and why?

_____

_____

_____

_____

_____

CHAPTER 4

The Castle: Home Sweet Home

Psalm 40:2 (NKJV)

"He also brought me up out of a horrible pit,
Out of the miry clay,
And set my feet upon a rock,
And established my steps."

In the story of *The Three Little Pigs*, one of the pigs built his house with hay and the Big Bad Wolf blew down his house. Hay blows in the wind unless it's tied together in a bale of hay. And even then, pieces of hay blow out of the tie that contains it. To me, this represents "every wind of doctrine" that is referenced in Ephesians 4. Everyone knows that in building structures, it is important to have a firm foundation.

My church sent a team to Thailand on a mission trip where the men worked on building the foundation for a ministry training center in Chiang Mai. The building is eventually going to be three stories high, so the foundation for this building must be firm and sure or it will not be safe and steady.

It is the same with our lives. We must lay a firm foundation so that we are not tossed to and fro by every wind of doctrine. We must be steady and firm on what we believe so that when contradictions and distractions come our way, we can stand strong.

Ephesians 4:11-16 (NKJV) says,

> *"And He Himself gave some to be apostles, some prophets, some evangelists, and some pastors and teachers, ¹² for the equipping of the saints for the work of ministry, for the edifying of the body of Christ, ¹³ till we all come to the unity of the faith and of the knowledge of the Son of God, to a perfect man, to the measure of the stature of the fullness of Christ; that we should no longer be children, tossed to and fro and carried about with every wind of doctrine, by the trickery of men, in the cunning craftiness of deceitful plotting, but, speaking the truth in love, may grow up in all things into Him who is the head—Christ—from whom the whole body, joined and knit together by what every joint supplies, according to the effective working by which every part does its share, causes growth of the body for the edifying of itself in love."*

Notice in verse 13 it says, "to a perfect man." That word "perfect" means mature. So as the apostles, prophets, evangelists, pastors, and teachers are doing their job equipping the saints (that's us), we are to be working toward coming to the unity of the faith and knowledge of the Son of God, becoming more mature to the measure of the stature (the height) of the fullness of Christ. When we do this, we will no longer be tossed around like children by every wind of doctrine. It specifically says "by the trickery of men, in the cunning craftiness of deceitful plotting."

While you are going about your business being a good Christian doing your good work, pay attention to what is going on around you, or else you will be blown around to and fro by some doctrine that isn't quite right or you may be distracted by the things of the world. It says "cunning craftiness of deceitful plotting." We must always be diligent and on target with keeping our foundation strong.

Reading and meditating on the Word of God will keep you diligent in your spiritual walk as you build layer upon layer on your spiritual foundation. Building your house on the Word of God will keep your foundation strong. No one will be able to blow your house down with cunning deceitfulness because you will be prepared for any wind or storm.

This makes me think of David and Goliath and what David fought the giant Goliath with. You may think that it was only the stone that brought that giant down, but it was the Word of God behind that stone that gave it the supernatural power to knock down the giant from the hand of a boy.

I Samuel 17:40 – 47 (NKJV),

"Then he took his staff in his hand; and he chose for himself five smooth stones from the brook, and put them in a shepherd's bag, in a pouch which he had, and his sling was in his hand. And he drew near to the Philistine. 41 So the Philistine came, and began drawing near to David, and the man who bore the shield went before him. 42 And when the Philistine looked about and saw David, he disdained him; for he was only a youth, ruddy and good-looking. 43 So the Philistine said to David, "Am I a dog, that you come to me with sticks?" And the Philistine cursed David by his gods. 44 And the Philistine said to David, "Come to me, and I will give your flesh to the birds of the air and the beasts of the field!"

The giant looked down on David because he was a boy. He disdained him because he was young and good-looking. David wasn't respected as a large trained soldier would have been. But David had something behind him that that giant did not have; this gave David the confidence to come out and challenge the giant. He knew he had the Almighty God with him and that gave him the confidence knowing that God would take care of the situation.

Sometimes we ladies are not respected because of our gender or our history or even our looks. Sometimes we are not given the same consideration as someone else for various reasons. But when we are walking out the will of God in our lives, we have Him and His power to back up what He wants us to do. He's the power behind our actions and words if we understand that He is with us. It gives us the confidence to pursue our dreams and to do the things that others may think we cannot or should not do.

Have you ever felt as though you were insignificant or not important enough to matter? How does this story of David and the giant speak to you?

_____

_____

_____

_____

_____

45 Then David said to the Philistine, "You come to me with a sword, with a spear, and with a javelin. But I come to you in the name of the LORD of hosts, the God of the armies of Israel, whom you have defied. 46 This day the LORD will deliver you into my hand, and I will strike you and take your head from you. And this day I will give the carcasses of the camp of the Philistines to the birds of the air and the wild beasts of the earth, that all the earth may know that there is a God in Israel. [47] Then all this assembly shall know that the LORD does not save with sword and spear; for the battle is the LORD's, and He will give you into our hands."

David spoke words of truth that the Lord was to deliver the giant into the hands of this boy. He said that he would strike him down. He knew that he was doing it through the strength and power of his mighty God. It may have looked like all he had for a weapon was a few smooth stones, but what David had for a weapon was the Word of God and the power behind that.

When you are battling in the spirit realm, the Word of God is the most powerful weapon you have. You may think it is only words, but those Words spoke this world into existence. Those Words healed the sick and split the Red Sea. Those Words brought down the walls of Jericho with a shout and calmed the sea. Those Words are sharper than a two-edged sword and are mightier than any weapon imagined.

The Word says that our enemies are not flesh and blood but spiritual entities. Ephesians 6:12 (NKJV) is clear on this,

> *"For we do not wrestle against flesh and blood, but against princi-palities, against powers, against the rulers of the darkness of this age against spiritual hosts of wickedness in the heavenly places."*

If we can keep in mind that our battles are spiritual, we will remember to go to the Word of God and prayer first to take on the battle. The Lord is our strength and He has given us the weapons to fight these battles—the Word of God and prayer.

We have more than stones, or even swords, to fight with. We have the Word of God. We have the Name of Jesus.

It says in John 14:12 (NKJV),

"Most assuredly, I say to you, he who believes in Me, the works that I do he will do also; and greater works than these he will do, because I go to My Father. [13] And whatever you ask in My name, that I will do, that the Father may be glorified in the Son.
[14] If you ask anything in My name, I will do it."

Remember, our battle is not physical but spiritual, therefore we must fight in the spirit. That is through the Word and in the Name of Jesus. Let's not come to the Word last when we are faced with a battle. Don't let the Word be a last-minute chance for a change in a situation. It must be our first response, our initial attack, our immediate answer in our time of need. It says here to ask in Jesus' Name. That is the ticket, the password, if you will.

He doesn't say here that we need to promise Him anything in exchange for Him answering our prayers. Many people seem to think that that will get our prayers answered quicker. But He only instructs us to ask and believe. It almost seems too simple. Surely there's more to it than that? Surely, He asks more of us than that? No, He asks us to trust Him, to ask and believe. Now in Mark 11, it also says that we must speak.

Mark 11:23 (NKJV) says,

"For assuredly, I say to you, whoever says to this mountain, 'Be removed and be cast into the sea,' and does not doubt in his heart, but believes that those things he says will be done, he will have whatever he says."

Whatever your mountain is, speak to it! It has to bow to the Name of Jesus. If your mountain is illness, use the Word to speak to that illness. If your mountain is a relationship, you speak to that situation through the Word. Whatever your mountain is, the Word is the answer.

Find a scripture that addresses your situation. Write it down on index cards or post-it notes and stick them to your mirror, on your refrigerator, or somewhere you will see it every day, and speak to that situation with the Word. And I mean speak it out loud. Every time you see it, you speak it out loud. That's why I say to put those post-it notes or index cards all over the house. Because seeing it over and over again and speaking it over and over again, builds your faith and that is first building your foundation and then building layers upon layers on that foundation.

Faith comes by hearing the Word of God. (Romans 10:17) That word "hearing" in the Greek is indicating a continuous verb. So in this scripture, it is saying that faith comes by hearing and hearing and hearing, etc. Your faith will grow each time you speak the Word of God.

David reminded himself of the times the Lord helped him defeat the lion and the bear to protect his sheep. So, remind yourself of the times He has come to your aid. Name them here and then meditate on them. They will encourage you.

_____

_____

_____

_____

_____

God has set our feet upon a rock, and then we are to build our foundation up with the Word. Part of the foundation is the footers. They must be dug deep into the ground for stability. Digging deep into the foundation of the Word is how we will stand through any storm. Having a solid foundation is the beginning and then layering your foundation with the Word to make you strong enough to withstand any storm that comes your way brings a victorious life.

Does that mean trials and tribulations never come our way? No, but it means that we can withstand the storms just like a strongly built structure.

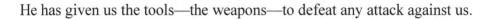

He has given us the tools—the weapons—to defeat any attack against us.

After digging our footers with the Word of God, we must build the foundation with layers of more truth, which is the Word of God. We must make sure to stay in the Word and, when we have a strong foundation to build upon, we will not be tossed to and fro. We will not have our house blown down because our foundation, walls, roof, windows, and doors are all solid and strong; nothing will take them down.

When your foundation is built on the Word of God and all the layers are only the Word of God, then there will be no wind of doctrine that can come along and blow you around. Opinion is not what a strong structure is made of. Man-made religious rules are not what constitutes a sturdy building. If the Word does not say it, don't believe it. It is that simple. When you know the Word of God, you will not be deceived by something that is not of God.

Your home, your castle, will be a strong fortress to stand against any wind of doctrine and all spiritual attacks that come against you and your family. It doesn't mean no attacks will ever happen. It means that you will have the foundation to stand against the storms and that you will have the appropriate weapons to fight against any attacks. You can even take the offensive and not live your life on the defense.

And remember this: Our battle is a spiritual battle. And your home is a castle able to withstand any attacks because you have built a strong foundation on the Word of God.

1. Read Ephesians 6:12 again and explain what it means and how it affects your life.

_____

_____

_____

_____

_____

2. What does the phrase "every wind of doctrine" mean and how can you make sure that you are not being tossed to and fro?

_____

_____

_____

_____

_____

3. How can you build your house on a solid foundation? What changes can you make in your life to assure that you are laying solid layers over your foundation?

_____

_____

_____

_____

_____

4. What scripture stood out to you when you read this chapter? Explain why.

_____

_____

_____

_____

_____

CHAPTER 5

It's All About the Dress

Ps 139:13- 16 (NIV)

"For you created my inmost being;
you knit me together in my mother's womb.
I praise you because I am fearfully and wonderfully made;
your works are wonderful, I know that full well.
My frame was not hidden from you
when I was made in the secret place,
when I was woven together in the depths of the earth.
Your eyes saw my unformed body;
all the days ordained for me were written in your book
before one of them came to be."

Kylee, our oldest granddaughter, came to the house one day and I was going on and on about how cute she looked. "That is a cute outfit, blah, blah, blah." Then DeeDa (my husband and her grandfather) came in and started telling her the same kinds of things, "You look so cute today", "That is a cute outfit." Kylee paused and put her arms around her DeeDa and said, "Maybe I was just born cute."

That is the way every child comes into this world. Whether the circumstances of the child's life are good or bad, they are oblivious to it and life is good. They are sweet, perfect, and happy. The struggles of this world have not tainted their self-image.

Anita Renfro, a Christian comedian, made an astute observation. She said that her children are flawed, deeply flawed. And the people they married are flawed, but for some reason they made perfect grandchildren. My husband and I raised three sons and so far, we have only granddaughters. I've noticed that granddaughters are perfect. They can do no wrong. Okay, maybe that is stretching it a little bit, but I do tend to be less tough on them than the boys. The boys are always saying we are too easy on the granddaughters.

But that also makes me think of our Heavenly Father and how he sees us. He sees us that way too. We are perfect in His eyes. As long as we have Jesus in our heart, He sees us under the blood. And sinners, He loves unconditionally as well, doing everything He can to draw them to Him so that He can have fellowship with them.

Ps 139:13- 16 (NIV)

"For you created my inmost being;
you knit me together in my mother's womb.
I praise you because I am fearfully and wonderfully made;
your works are wonderful,
I know that full well.
My frame was not hidden from you
when I was made in the secret place,
when I was woven together in the depths of the earth.

Your eyes saw my unformed body;
all the days ordained for me were written in your book
before one of them came to be."

We all have a story, and everyone's story begins here. Psalm 139:13-16 gives us a glimpse into each person's beginning. Not everyone is aware of or living out this fact, but it still remains true. Our beginning is with God. He says He knitted each one of us together in our mother's womb. He was present in our very beginning, which is even before our beginning on this earth. We are fearfully and wonderfully made. Our frame is not hidden means that He could see us and that His eyes saw our unformed bodies while we were growing in our mother's womb.

And look at this part, "All the days ordained for me were written in your book before one of them (my ordained days) came to be." He knew who I was and what I would be doing each day of my life. My days are already written in HIS book before they happened. He knew me and He loved me before I could even know who He was or what He could do for me. It also says in that scripture that His works are wonderful and you and I are creations of His, part of His works.

As young children, it is easy to believe that we are fearfully and wonder-fully made. When Kylee was younger, she had no self-image issues. A few years ago when she was about six years old, Mike, Kylee and I were get-ting our things together to walk out the door to go somewhere, and Kylee ran up to DeeDa and hugged him around his legs, and said "Aren't I just so sweet?" Because that's what we always told her and she believed it.

But since then, she has experienced some of the "mean girl" stuff starting in the first grade. She has already had girls saying ugly things to her. We as parents and grandparents have an influence in their lives. We are a picture of the Heavenly Father, so we should be encouraging them and saying positive things because we know that there will be plenty of people in the world who will try to knock them down a notch or two every chance they get.

We should understand that God was in the beginning of our forming and that He had a hand in creating who we are. We are His. We are children of the Living God and no matter what comes our way or what people say about us, we can walk with our heads held high and our shoulders back with confidence because of Whose we are. We need to believe what our Heavenly Father says about us; not what others say or think about us.

Not everyone has wonderful beginning stories. Some are raised in homes that are not encouraging and happy. Some have had to go through some terrible situations. And then some of us have had tough things that we go through in this life as we get older. None of these things take away from whom God made us to be. We are fearfully and wonderfully made.

Has your self-image been warped by the world or by some other person's opinion of you?

_____

_____

_____

_____

_____

There is a great analogy in the story of Cinderella. The newest movie version of this story came out a few years ago and our women's ministry happened to be in Mexico at the time the movie came to the theaters. We were working at an orphanage that we visit every summer. As an outing with the children, we took the children to the movie theater and this new moving was showing. The only problem was that it was in Spanish.

Well, we really did not see any problem because we are so familiar with the story that we just watched it even though we did not understand the language. This was actually a very beautiful experience. Watching this movie without words was mesmerizing. It was beautifully done and I could concentrate on the visual aspects of the story.

So here is what I saw: Cinderella had a great childhood with a loving mother and father. Everything was going great, and she enjoyed life. You could tell from the facial expressions of this little family that they were very happy. Then, suddenly, it all changed. First, she lost her mother but she was left with a loving and caring father. Those years spent together as father and daughter were special. They loved each other and built a life of love and caring.

When her father remarried and then died, she was left with a bitter and hateful woman who mistreated and abused her. But she continued to walk in joy no matter her circumstances because she had developed a sweet and caring spirit during the years of growing up first with her mother and father, and then with just her dad. She worked hard to not be bitter. But she finally reached a point when she felt as though she couldn't take anymore. The night of the ball, she broke down and asked for help.

There are times when we become frustrated and downhearted. Or as in my case, I realized at age twenty, I wasn't going to heaven if I didn't make a huge change in my life. I had to surrender my life to Jesus and allow Him to become my Savior. Whatever we are going through, Luke 4:18-19 has the answer. Let's see what the Lord says about our story:

Luke 4:18-19 (NKJV) says,

*"The Spirit of the Lord is on me,
because he has anointed me
to proclaim good news to the poor.
He has sent me to proclaim freedom for the prisoners
and recovery of sight for the blind,
to set the oppressed free,
[19] to proclaim the year of the Lord's favor."*

and verse 20 says, *"Then He closed the book, and gave it back to the attendant and sat down. And the eyes of all who were in the synagogue were fixed on Him. 21 And He began to say to them, "Today this Scripture is fulfilled in your hearing."*

What scripture is He talking about? He is referring to the Old Testament prophecy and he reads it in the synagogue:

And Isaiah 61:1-3 (NKJV),

"The Spirit of the Lord GOD is upon Me,
Because the LORD has anointed Me
To preach good tidings to the poor;
He has sent Me to [a]heal the brokenhearted,"

Most of the time, we stop here. We focus and memorize this scripture. But let's look at the rest.

"To proclaim liberty to the captives,
And the opening of the prison to those who are bound;
2 To proclaim the acceptable year of the Lord,
And the day of vengeance of our God;
To comfort all who mourn,
3 To [b]console those who mourn in Zion,
To give them beauty for ashes,
The oil of joy for mourning,
The garment of praise for the spirit of heaviness; ..."

Our Heavenly Father was thinking of us before we were ever born. He had the answer for us before we had the question. He had a plan for us before we knew we needed one. Look at what this covers: poor, brokenhearted, captives, and prisoners, and those who are mourning and who are in despair. When we finally realize that we need a savior, that is the moment of despair until we make Jesus our savior. As it says in Luke 4:20, Jesus is the fulfillment of these scriptures. He is the fulfillment of the answer to anything that comes up in our lives. But we first must make Him our savior so that He can work in our lives.

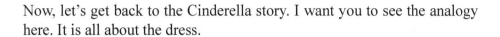

Now, let's get back to the Cinderella story. I want you to see the analogy here. It is all about the dress.

In the Cinderella story, after she had cried out for help on the night of the ball and after the fairy godmother had turned the mice into horsemen and horses to pull the carriage made from the pumpkin, she looks at Cinderella and realizes that Cinderella needs a new dress. But Cinderella tells the fairy godmother that she wants to wear her mother's dress, and if she could just fix it and clean it up, that would be just fine.

That's what we do. We don't want to ask for too much. We might be considered selfish. Or we already have a plan and we just want God to go along with it. We do not want God to do something new. We want Him to take our old plan and just rework it to make it a little better. But God has a much better plan than that and if we will wait on Him and let Him make a new plan, we will be walking out our destiny to the fullest.

Have you ever asked God to work out your plan? How did that turn out?

_____

_____

_____

_____

_____

Cinderella wanted to hold onto something from her past. She wanted to continue in the past. This was her mother's dress. There is nothing wrong with honoring our past as long as it does not keep us from moving forward in God's plan for our lives. God wants us to put away the old man, put away the past, so that we can look to the future, the future and purpose for which He has created us.

In this version of the story, the fairy godmother convinced Cinderella that she needed a new dress. So, when the fairy godmother transformed the dress to the new one, Cinderella could not have imagined a more beautiful dress. We cannot always imagine the purpose and plan God has for us. We think that we know what our abilities and skills are and what we are capable of doing, but God sometimes has another destiny for us, one that we would have never dreamed of ourselves.

Romans 12:2 in the New Living Translation says,

"Don't copy the behavior and customs of this world, but let God transform you into a new person by changing the way you think. Then you will learn to know God's will for you, which is good and pleasing and perfect."

Just like Cinderella eventually allowed her fairy godmother to create her dress, a dress that Cinderella could not have dreamed up or created herself, we need to leave it to our Heavenly Father to design the plan for our lives and then allow the Holy Spirit to lead and guide us to execute it. Learn to know God's will, which is good and pleasing and perfect. We want His perfect will. We could have a decent life and we could be doing our plan and God can bless it to a certain level, but being in the perfect will of God is living a life that we could not have dreamed up ourselves.

Ephesians 4:22-24 says it like this in the NIV,

"You were taught, with regard to your former way of life, to put off your old self, which is being corrupted by its deceitful desires; [23] to be made new in the attitude of your minds; [24] and to put on the new self, created to be like God in true righteousness and holiness."

Cinderella was going to settle for her mother's old dress, but her fairy godmother had a better plan, just as God has a better plan for us. Her fairy godmother designed a dress that was so beautiful that it took the Prince's breath away and captured the attention of everyone at the ball. Cinderella could not have created anything like that. It is the same way with God.

He has a plan and purpose for each one of us and, if we will allow Him to clothe us as a new creature and design our plan, we will be walking out the perfect will for our lives. We can follow our plan and receive some blessings, but to live out the plan that God has given us, will bring full blessings that we will not be able to contain.

Are you holding on to an old dress (plan) in your life?

_____

_____

_____

_____

_____

The Amplified Version says Roman 12:2 this way:

"And do not be conformed to this world [any longer with its superficial values and customs], but be transformed and progressively changed [as you mature spiritually] by the renewing of your mind [focusing on godly values and ethical attitudes], so that you may prove [for yourselves] what the will of God is, that which is good and acceptable and perfect [in His plan and purpose for you]."

When we are trying to do life in our own might and our own strength, we conform to what the world dictates as successful. But if you are renewing your mind in the Word of God and seeking His will, you will follow His plan for your life: His good, pleasing, and perfect will.

Cinderella's mother's dress was very pretty for the older time period. But it was out of date and out of style. But the new dress that was created was more beautiful than Cinderella could even imagine. She was more beautiful than she could even imagine herself to be.

We can try to create our life and God can bless it to a point, but if we allow Him to make those plans, if we would look to Him for the purpose and plan for our lives, He can make our lives the beautiful plan that He desires for our lives. As humans, we have a finite mind. We cannot see into the future. If we would leave our plans in God's hands, He could make something more beautiful than we could even imagine.

Ephesians 2:10 (NIV)

"For we are God's handiwork, created in Christ Jesus to do good works, which God prepared in advance for us to do."

This tells me that when He first knew me—which was in my mother's womb—He had a plan that He had prepared for me in advance to fulfill. Do you think that you have made wrong decisions that took you out of God's perfect plan? My answer to that is that God already knew that you would do those things and make those decisions. I believe He takes into account what He knows we will do.

Does He want us to make all the right decisions in our lives? Sure, He does. But He also gave us free will and with that, we sometimes blow it and do the wrong thing. That does not take us out of the plan He has for us. He was not surprised by those choices. He still expects us to fulfill the plan and purpose that He has arranged for us in advance, and it is our responsibility to walk it out in our lives.

To live up to our potential as a princess in the Royal Family of God is the result of following His plan for our lives. Do we get every step perfect? No. Does a performer make mistakes? Does a ball player make errors? Does the CEO make a bad marketing decision? Sure, those things happen, but as long as we are listening to His voice in our planning and not the world, He will honor our attempts. He is a gracious and merciful God.

So, let God create your beautiful dress. Give Him creative license to design a full and satisfied life plan for you so that you will be doing His will and living up to your potential.

1. Are you settling for an old dress when you could be wearing the new dress God has for you? Name a dream that you have had in your heart.

_____

_____

_____

_____

_____

2. What has distracted you from fulfilling this dream? Name them here and state what you can do to change this.

_____

_____

_____

_____

3. What decisions in your life do you need to make for which you should seek God's will?

_____

_____

_____

_____

_____

4. What scripture helped you to see that you are God's creation?

_____

_____

_____

_____

_____

CHAPTER 6

You Can Never Have Too Many Shoes

Ephesians 6:13-17 (NKJV)

"Therefore take up the whole armor of God, that you may be able to withstand in the evil day, and having done all, to stand.
Stand therefore, having girded your waist with truth, having put on the breastplate of righteousness, and having shod your feet with the preparation of the gospel of peace; above all, taking the shield of faith with which you will be able to quench all the fiery darts of the wicked one. And take the helmet of salvation, and the sword of the Spirit, which is the word of God;"

A few years ago I did a message on this "taking up the whole armor of God", and I had borrowed a fireman's whole set of gear. So, for each part, I put on the corresponding garment or equipment that firemen don for fighting fires. It was a fun sermon, and I thoroughly enjoyed putting on the equipment and making the spiritual connection to each piece of equipment. It certainly relayed the idea of putting on the whole armor of God as if putting on protective gear.

It also demonstrated that we are to be doing the action. When the scripture says to "take up," it has the assumed subject of "you." So it is really saying, "you take up" the whole armor of God. The action is to be done by us. God has done all that He needs to. We need to understand our part in this life of faith.

When we are talking about taking up -- or it could be said putting on -- the whole armor of God before we leave the house, you could actually think about it as putting on protective gear. We are protecting ourselves from being influenced or corrupted by the world that we must live in and to be active members of the Royal Kingdom of God.

First we see in verse13 that we are told – not asked or suggested – but told to take up the whole armor of God. We are to take each piece and put it in place. It does not say to wait for God to put it on us. We are told to do it. God would not tell us to do something in the Word that we did not have the ability do. It is an action that we can and are expected to perform.

In that same verse 13 it also gives us the reason to put on the whole armor of God – so that you may withstand in the evil day and, having done all, to stand. He has given us the tools by which we can withstand the evil that we are tempted with in this world and also the strength and ability to stand against any battle that comes our way. We've already established that our battles are not physical but spiritual. This tells us how we can prepare and win the spiritual battle that we come up against when we leave our home each day.

Verse 14 says that our waist must be girded with truth. Another word for gird is to surround or encircle. So the statement says "Surround yourself with truth." Where do we get truth? The Word of God. There are a lot of things that are true in the world, but the Word of God is truth, and it is steadfast and sure. To surround yourself with the Word of God is to protect you from deception and deception is the only tool of our enemy. If you have truth to wipe out deception, then there is nothing else that the enemy can defeat you with.

The second half of verse 14 names the breastplate of righteousness. Righteousness means right standing with God. The breastplate of a suit of armor protects the chest area where the heart and lungs are. Think about that! The right standing we have with God through our salvation that came from the blood of Jesus not only protects our heart, which pumps the life blood through us, but it also protects our lungs, in which the Lord breathed life into us.

As in Genesis 2:7 when God breathed into Adam, Jesus breathed life onto the disciples in John 20:22 to sent them out to do ministry. We are commissioned to do that as well and with God's blessing and Jesus's commission, we have the breastplate of righteousness to protect our heart and lungs.

The shield of faith, it says in verse 16, with which you will quench all fiery darts from the evil one is important for you to hold steady against the deception that I mentioned before. The enemy's only weapon against us is deception, and notice that the scripture says that you will quench all fiery darts by holding up the shield of faith. Once again, the scripture is instructing us that we are to be doing the action of holding the shield of faith. Gaining the knowledge of faith will give us the steadiness of holding that shield against attacks.

Verse 17 mentions the helmet of salvation. What part of the body does a helmet go on? The head – to protect the head, the skull, the brain, the mind. This tells me that the mind has to be protected. Once again we are speaking spiritually as we have determined that these are spiritual battles.

After salvation our mind has to be renewed to come in line with the Word of God. When we ask Jesus to become our Savior and we are born again, our spirit is immediately transformed. But our mind and body take time to make the change. They have been influenced by the world for however long we have been without a savior, and the mind and body do not make immediate transformation like the spirit does.

This is why the helmet of salvation is so important. We are to read, study, and meditate on the Word of God for the transformation of our mind so that we can bring our body into transformation as well. I like the way the New Living Translation says Romans 12:2:

"Don't copy the behavior and customs of this world, but let God transform you into a new person by changing the way you think. Then you will learn to know God's will for you, which is good and pleasing and perfect."

In the second part of verse 17, the sword of the Spirit is named and that is the Word of God. The Word of God "is alive and powerful. It is sharper than the sharpest two-edged sword." (Hebrews 4:12)

What changes can you make in the morning to help you to put on your armor of God before you leave the house?

_____

_____

_____

_____

_____

If you didn't notice, I skipped the feet being shod with the gospel of peace as I was going through this section of scripture. That's because our focus in this chapter is specifically about verse 15 where it says, *"and having shod your feet with the preparation of the gospel of peace"* as it is said in the New King James Version but I didn't want to just skip over all the other parts of the armor.

Now we are going to concentrate on the feet because you know … "you can never have too many shoes." I bet you are wondering what in the world I mean by that. You'll find out soon enough. Let's dig right in to what the Word says about our feet:

The New Living Translation says it this way, *"For shoes, put on the peace that comes from the Good News so that you will be fully prepared."* Fully prepared for what? We will get to that.

Now, ladies, we know that shoes are important to a woman. There are different shoes for different purposes. We decide on a pair of shoes depending on weather, the activities of the day, and what matches what we are wearing. We put a lot of thought into what shoes to wear on any given day.

There are shoes that you know you can wear all day, and there are shoes that you know you cannot wear all day. We have work shoes and play shoes. We have shoes for going out on the town and shoes for staying in. We have shoes that we walk in and shoes that we exercise in. There is a definite decision that has to be made about your shoes each day.

My husband and I have had this conversation many times. He cannot figure out why I have to take several shoes on a trip. He takes one pair of tennis shoes and one pair of casual or dress shoes that he can wear with either khakis, jeans, or dress pants—whichever is called for depending on the scheduled activities. It is just not the same for women. It comes down to purpose.

Let's look back at Ephesians 6:15 in the Living Bible. It says *"wear shoes that will speed you on..."* for your purpose *"... which is to spread the*

Good News of the peace of God. "

Now let's give that some thought:

Once again, we are down to "purpose." What is our purpose in this scripture? It says we must wear shoes so that we can spread the Good News of the peace of God. The New Living Translation says, "…so that you will be fully prepared." Prepared for what? Prepared for our purpose: To spread the Good News of the gospel of peace.

It says in verse 14 in the New English Translation, *"Stand firm therefore,"* in verse 15, *"...by fitting your feet with the preparation that comes from the good news of peace. "*

We all know that the right fit makes a huge difference in wearing your shoes. You can't just buy any old pair without considering the fit and size. Fitting is specific for everyone, just as our calling is specific. We are not all called to do the same thing in the Kingdom of God. There are planters, waterers, and reapers. What I mean by that is that there are people who plant a seed-thought about Jesus to someone, then someone else comes along and waters that seed, and then eventually, someone leads that person to Jesus. Each one had a part in that person's story. We all have a part to play in building and growing the Kingdom of God.

There are various walks of life. There is the business world and the world of fitness. There is the stay-at-home mom and the working mom. There is the teenager and the elderly. All of these ladies have people with whom they come in contact.

Who do you fit with? Who do you connect with in your daily walk? Who do you rub shoulders with that you can influence? We all have a purpose and that is to reach people with the good news as it says in Ephesians 6:15. When we are walking through our lives, we are touching people every day. Are we influencing them toward God or away from God? It is one or the other. Just as our shoes are specific for purpose and fit, so is our part in the Kingdom of God.

What walk of life do you fit into? Who do you rub shoulders with?

_____

_____

_____

_____

_____

1 Corinthians 12:12 (NKJV)

"For as the body is one and has many members, but all the members of that one body, being many, are one body, so also is Christ."

Verse 20

"But now indeed there are many members, yet one body."

Once we are born again and enter the Royal Family of God, we all have a part in its function. It is the body of Christ and each one of us has a special duty or task. What we are to do for our Lord is personal and specific for each of us. We are to be led by the Holy Spirit to find our purpose and place in the Kingdom, just like trying on shoes for the purpose for which we are choosing them. We should not be looking to someone else to copy their part in the Kingdom. We are expected to find our own specific place in the Kingdom of God.

I am enamored with people who can sing and play instruments, and, if I'm not careful, I'll be caught up wishing that I could lead worship like someone else does. But then I have to remind myself that God did not create me that way. He created me for something else.

Have you ever found yourself comparing yourself to someone else? How does that make you feel?

_____

_____

_____

_____

_____

Your influence is going to be in the circles in which you run. You don't need to try to be someone you are not to be the influence to which God has called you. You be you and God will do the rest.

I don't need a high-heeled boot if I'm going hiking in the woods. I need the appropriate boot. God leads us by His Holy Spirit to go through our day making decisions and making a difference in the lives of others. When we wake up in the morning and we try to decide what to wear, we should also be aware that we are going out into the world to be a light to the world.

Being led by the Spirit comes from waking up each day aware and alert to hear His voice. What are we wearing? Are we wearing the shoes that are appropriate for that day to spread the Good News of peace? When I mean "shoes" here, I mean purpose, attitude, and awareness. Awareness of a fallen world who needs the message of the Good News of peace.

Now let's go back up to verse 10-13 of Ephesians 6,

"Finally, be strong in the Lord and in his mighty power. Put on the full armor of God, so that you can take your stand against the devil's schemes. For our struggle is not against flesh and blood, but against the *rulers, against the authorities, against the powers of this dark world and against the spiritual forces of evil in the heavenly realms. Therefore put on the full armor of God, so that when the day of evil comes, you may be able to stand your ground, and after you have done everything, to stand."*

Notice that this is talking about the spiritual battle that goes on. I covered this in a previous chapter, but it is significant here as well. This is a spiritual battle, so when we prepare to go out into the world, whether it is to work, to school, or to functions where we have to rub up against people who do not call Jesus their Savior, we need to be led by the Spirit. We need to have on our whole armor including our shoes with the gospel of peace.

Romans 8:14 (NLT) says,

"For all who are led by the Spirit of God are children of God."

We have established and will continue to reiterate that we are children of the Living God, princesses in the Royal Family of God. So this is what we do: We are led by the Spirit of God. To be led by the Holy Spirit as we are instructed, we must begin our day with the awareness of His presence and His promptings. When we put on each piece of our armor, the shoes of the gospel of peace is one of the things that the world needs to see in us.

No matter what is going on in our personal lives and in the world in general, they need to see that we are walking in a supernatural peace that only God can give us. It comes from the Holy Spirit and the confidence that we are being led by the Holy Spirit.

We have so much more to offer people than the world's concepts and beliefs, but if we are not showing the peace that surpasses all understand (Philippians 4:7 NKJV), then we are not making a difference in people's lives. Being led by the Spirit is to listen for those small nudgings that lead us to speak to someone who needs an encouraging word or to cover someone's grocery bill in line at the store.

People should see the peace of God that permeates our lives and if they are not seeing this from His disciples, then what do we have to offer the ones who need that nurturing, that hope, that peace that can help them through the toughest times of their lives?

It says in Isaiah 52:7 (NLT):

*"How beautiful on the mountains are the feet of the messenger who brings good news, the good news of peace
and salvation, the news that the God of Israel reigns!"*

You are that messenger to the world. Your beauty comes from the Holy Spirit who gives us joy and peace through salvation. Wherever you walk on this earth, you take Jesus with you and if you share your joy and peace with others, you make a difference in people's lives. I hear people say that they want to make a difference all the time. You are making a difference everyday just being you, the you that God created with the joy and peace that can only come from Him. If people are seeing that in you, you are making a difference.

They will know who to come to when they need encouragement and prayer. Keep that in mind as you go through your day. Walk through your life with purpose, knowing that you are a princess in the Royal Family of God and that you can bring light and joy and peace to others, for we have the answers of life through our Lord Jesus Christ.

So, each morning as you choose your clothing and your shoes, be aware of your purpose for that day, which is to carry the gospel of peace to the world that you touch each day. Be aware of the Holy Spirit inside of you that leads you to walk that peace out. Be intentional in your connections with people each day. Be prepared to spread the Gospel of peace to your fellow man. Be led to wear the appropriate shoes, the appropriate attitude and purpose that will be what that person will need for that day.

1. What does your typical day look like? Who do you interact with each day and how can you influence them?

_____

_____

_____

_____

_____

2. Is there a person or two who you can target that you can bring the gospel of peace to in your speech and actions?

_____

_____

_____

_____

3. What kinds of things are going on in your life that you must call on God for a supernatural peace to help you make it through the day? How can this relate to interacting with others in your day-to-day life?

_____

_____

_____

_____

4. What scripture from this chapter spoke to you? And why?

_____

_____

_____

_____

_____

CHAPTER 7

Unpack your Royal Baggage

Ecclesiastes 3:11 NKJV

"He has made everything beautiful in its time."

We all love going on trips. Long trips, short trips. Trips for vacation or to visit family. Business or pleasure. Every once in a while, we have a sad trip, perhaps to a funeral, but even those can be fun as you have an opportunity to relive memories of the deceased with friends and family. But overall, trips are interesting and fun. They take us somewhere other than home, away from our everyday lives.

After a trip, do you immediately empty your bags and put everything away? Do you do it a little at a time? Or does it sometimes take days to get it all unloaded? Whether we empty it immediately or take a while to do it, we often find that something was left behind.

How many of us leave stuff behind in our handbags? There are times when I have been looking for something and finally find it in a purse that I thought I emptied when I was transferring to another purse or tote. What kinds of things do we leave behind? Sometimes those are small items, like a nail file or a receipt. But sometimes those small items can have a big impact on our lives.

If we look at life like a trip, there are times when we have left things behind in our baggage that can cause real problems later in life. Some of the things that we leave in our purses or luggage can be big things. We think that if we don't see them, then they won't bother us.

We all have baggage when we come to Jesus. Don't be like the ostrich and bury it in the sand but don't be like the elephant and remember it forever. When we look at the things that we left behind, there are two things that we must do so that we can move forward in life and pursue the life that God intends for us.

First, we have to acknowledge that it is there, hidden away somewhere. We may have to spend some time in the Word to have the Holy Spirit reveal to us what is buried that is plaguing us. Sometimes we have trust issues because someone has failed us. We believe that we have moved on from it, but, if not dealt with, it could be bothering us in ways we do not recognize. We may have childhood memories that we are wanting to put to rest. God

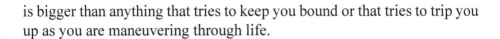

is bigger than anything that tries to keep you bound or that tries to trip you up as you are maneuvering through life.

Then, second, once we recognized that we have something that needs to be dealt with, we are to give it to God. God makes good come from whatever happens in our lives, but if we ignore it or leave it in the purse or bag to be out of sight, we can't work through it and move forward and away from it. We can't expect God to make something beautiful out of it if we won't look it in the eye to deal with it.

As it says in Ecclesiastes 3:11 (NKJV),

"He has made everything beautiful in its time."

Our Heavenly Father must be given the time and availability to do His work and, to do that work, He has to have access to the baggage so that He can make something beautiful out of it. Being in denial or pretending nothing happened in your life that has had an effect on you will hinder you from putting that thing behind you for good.

When we don't deal with it so that we can give it to Jesus, it will rear its ugly head up at times that could hurt a relationship or keep us from fulfilling God's plan in our lives. These kinds of things give us feelings of unworthiness or unacceptance, and this hinders us from taking proper steps away from it and toward a better choice.

My husband the lead pastor at our church reminds the congregation regularly that if someone is having a problem or has a need of some kind, someone needs to let the staff know. He will sometimes get an idea from the Holy Spirit that someone has a need, but we shouldn't leave it to that.

It's the same way with the Lord. Even though we know that God knows everything, He expects us to ask Him for what we need. As we learn to ask Him, trust is developed and strengthened.

At our church, we offer bible studies and groups for people who have gone through divorce. There are some people who know that they need this to get past the devastation of divorce. But it is amazing to me how many people will not attend any kind of class, support group, or bible study on this subject. They feel that they are over it and that they don't need help, but we as pastors find that later these same people have trouble moving on to healthy relationships. There are hurt feelings and trust issues that will continue to plague them if they do not get help from people who are prepared to assist them through these issues. God will help them work through these, but they have to be willing to ask for help.

Ecclesiastes 3 also says in verse 6,

"A time to gain,
And a time to lose;
A time to keep,
And a time to throw away;"

Think about what this is saying to us. There is a time to gain and the way to gain is to lose. Gain what? The full and abundant life God has chosen for you. Lose what? Those things that you may have left behind in the baggage of your life. This is also the time to keep what? All the promises God has for you. Throw away what? Those things that weigh you down and hold you back from moving forward in your full life with God, that keep you from challenging yourself in this walk with your Savior.

Let's make an exercise out of this. Stop right now and think about what you may have held onto or ignored. Pray and be led by the spirit. We all have something that we could be working on. Fill out the chart below and let's be specific so that we can ask God to take away the things that are dragging us down and to hold onto the things that will help us propel forward:

SOMETHING TO GAIN	SOMETHING TO LOSE
_____	_____
_____	_____
_____	_____
_____	_____
_____	_____

SOMETHING TO KEEP	SOMETHING TO THROW AWAY
_____	_____
_____	_____
_____	_____
_____	_____

Our God is the God of second chances. But we can't stop at just salvation and knowing who God is. There is so much more to what comes with our relationship with God. And if we don't pursue all that He has for us, we could be right back where we were—carrying our baggage again.

What we have to do is believe who He says we are. We have to believe in our position and our rights as a child of the Living God, as a princess in the Kingdom of God. The way to be able to do that is to be free of the stuff that has been collecting in our baggage.

When I travel and take a plane to go somewhere, I make the choice to check my luggage so that I don't have to lug that around the airport and have to put it up in the hold above the seats in the plane. That is a personal choice of mine. Many people choose to carry their small bags on the plane, but to me it is cumbersome and irritating.

Imagine someone going through the airport with a small piece of luggage maneuvering around people, stopping at a store to pick up a snack for the plane, or stopping at one of the food vendors to grab a bite to take on the plane or eat before she gets on the plane. She is calmly taking care of business waiting on her plane and keeping up with her small carry-on.

Now, picture the scene when she realizes that she has lost track of time. She has to get to the gate quickly and has to drag the luggage with her quickly to the gate. All of a sudden, that luggage seems heavy and bothersome. While she was sitting down and leisurely eating her dinner while waiting on her flight, the luggage didn't seem to be a problem, but when she had to move quickly to get somewhere fast, that luggage became a problem.

It is the same with life. We can walk around with our baggage from past hurts and disappoints and they don't seem to bother us most of the time, but when it is time to move forward in a relationship or a time to fulfill a dream or goal, that baggage becomes like dead weight all of a sudden. We seem to get dragged down and then we have a difficult time making the right choices or even worse, we can't see ourselves finishing what we started.

Those things that we have left buried from the past can make us think we can't do something or that we are not worthy of the success we have the potential to experience. God makes everything good, but we have to give it to Him and let Him work those things out. We have to believe who He says we are in Him and let Him help us to move forward in life to see ourselves for who we are in His sight.

Take some time right now and think about what you might have left in some old baggage. What effect has it had on dreams or relationships?

_____

_____

_____

_____

_____

So, what are the things that you need to throw away? What are the things that you secretly have left behind in the baggage of your lives? God has the answer for anything that is keeping you from living an abundant life in Christ Jesus.

Remember, He takes the ugly in our lives and make it good:

- **Loneliness?** He took loneliness and said He would never leave us.
- **Shame?** He took shame and replaced it with honor.
- **Rejection?** He took rejection and accepted us into His family.
- **Hate?** He took hate and loved us unconditionally.
- **Greed?** He took greed and filled our lives with true riches.
- **Fear?** He took fear and gave us a sound mind.
- **Insignificance?** He took insignificance and gave us meaning and purpose.

Are there issues such as these in your life that are keeping you from living a life of freedom? Keeping you from fulfilling your God kind of life? Holding you back from pursuing your God-given purpose in life? Any of these can hold us back from allowing God to work in our lives to make things good out of bad. Understanding your relationship with your Heavenly Father and knowing that He only has good in store for you gives you the freedom to believe that He means what He says in the Bible. The Word of God is truth. What it says never changes.

Romans 8:28 in the NIV says,

> *"And we know that in all things God works for the good of those who love him, who have been called according to his purpose."*

Let's look at someone in the Bible who could have stayed in that undeserving mindset but chose to walk out of the circumstances in life to make a better life for her and her family. God did that for her, but she had to believe that God was willing to do that.

In the Book of Joshua Chapter 2, we read about Rahab who is in the lineage of Jesus. She is in the Royal Family of God, but she did not start off that way. Rahab is a very interesting woman and her life is evidence that there are "skeletons" in all of our ancestries.

We find, in Joshua 2, that Joshua—in his new position as leader of the Israelites—sent two spies into Jericho to spy out the land. The two spies hid out in a "harlot's" home; her name was Rahab. Now, how and why they ended up there, it does not say, but what we do know is that she hid them from the leaders of Jericho. Somehow, the king of Jericho found out and sent his men to get these spies. She misdirected them from her home to keep the Hebrew spies from being caught.

Now, let's look at Joshua Chapter 2, beginning at verse 9. This is where her faith kicks in.

In verse 9 she says to the spies,

> *"I know that the Lord has given you the land, that the terror of you has fallen on us, and that all the inhabitants of the land are fainthearted because of you."*

And here she proceeds to list the acts of God that she has heard that bring her people to fear Him and for her to believe that He is the one true God, as she testifies in verse 12,

"He is God in heaven above and on earth beneath."

This is where it becomes very interesting. She has the faith to ask for salvation not only for her, a harlot and enemy, but for all of her family. She lays her life before the representatives of the God in heaven above and on earth beneath and trusts all their lives to His promises. Now catch this next thing. In verse 17 through 20, the spies give her specific instructions so that her family will be saved from bloodshed. It says that when everything goes down, to tie a scarlet cord (which represents salvation through the blood) in the window and bring everyone into the house for safekeeping.

For a quick history lesson, the first time we see this is when Moses leads the Israelites from Egypt. God tells Moses to instruct the Israelites to bring all of their family into their homes and to put blood around their doors. This was the sign to spare these homes when the next and last curse came upon the Egyptians.

Then this same sign is implemented in Rahab's story of salvation. The Old Testament has many similar correlations and these are types and shadows of what was to come in the New Covenant that was created with Jesus and His death and resurrection. His blood wipes our sins away, and we are saved because of the blood.

The two instructions that Rahab was given are very important for us to understand. First is that a scarlet cord should be tied on the window which alerts the Hebrew army to pass it during the skirmish, and the second is that she must have everyone in the house to keep them safe.

Both of these have very significant parallels in the spirit. The scarlet cord represents the blood of Jesus that saves us and then to have everyone in the house is signifying that we are protected by God.

The Bible is explicit that we ought to be led by the Spirit and to live a righteous life. There are so many times that we are given instructions through the Holy Spirit as part of our faith walk to see the mighty hand of God working in our lives. And because Rahab did as she was told, rescuing her and her family was one of the first things Joshua commanded his men to do before destroying all of Jericho. This is found in Joshua 6:22-25.

How does this story effect you? Can you relate in any way to Rahab?

_____

_____

_____

_____

_____

What a wonderful story of a woman who grabbed hold of her opportunity to make a better life, and it began when she chose to believe that God would keep His promise. She took the risk to ask for help, to ask to be rescued, and she waited patiently for the rescue to happen.

Be sure to read this story of faith for yourself. Put yourself in her shoes. She must have had a lot of baggage to have the label of harlot but she knew the promise the spies had made to her. She followed their instructions, and she stood in faith waiting for her rescue. That baggage in her life did not keep her from asking for help. That baggage did not hold her back. She believed what she had heard of this God and chose to believe Him and, because of that, her life and the lives of her family were changed.

But her story does not end there:

In Hebrews 11:31 (NKJV), the chapter that I like to call the Hall of Faith, the Bible tells us,

"By faith the harlot Rahab did not perish with those who did not believe, when she had received the spies with peace."

Rahab is being singled out in the Hall of Faith as a person of faith because she believed what she had heard about God and put her trust in Him for her life and the lives of her family members.

But not only were Rahab and her family rescued from death and that she is listed in the Hall of Faith in Hebrews 11 with some of great faith people of the Bible, she was also of the lineage of David, which is the lineage of Jesus. It says it in Matthew 1:5 (NKJV),

*"Salmon begot Boaz by **Rahab**, Boaz begot Obed by Ruth, Obed begot Jesse"*

…where the lineage of Jesus is listed. It is also interesting to note that where this list is made, most of the women in the lineage are not mentioned, but Rahab and Ruth are because of the significant stories behind their lives. Rahab went from harlot to princess and it took her believing that God would fulfill His promise to her and her family. She was a member of the Royal Family of God, just like you are. God has promises for His children and you have the right to claim these promises in your life and to live a fulfilled life.

Do not let the baggage of your life keep you from the beautiful and fulfilling life God has for you. Let Him come and work on your behalf. Don't let that stuff linger back there in your past to play havoc on your future. Get it out and let God work. That is His specialty.

1. Do you have some stuff lingering in old luggage or used purses that you keep hidden? What can God do with that?

_____

_____

_____

_____

_____

2. What kind of life does God want for you? Close your eyes and visualize what that life can look like and ask God and believe that He wants what is good in your life. Write down what that looks like to you.

_____

_____

_____

_____

_____

3. How can you unload the baggage in your past to God so that He can work on your behalf? What can you do to walk out the life that God wants for you?

_____

_____

_____

_____

_____

4. What scripture in this chapter spoke to you and why?

_____

_____

_____

_____

_____

CHAPTER 8

The Role of a Princess

Romans 12:10 (NLT)

*Love each other with genuine affection,
and take delight in honoring each other.*

There is an old classic movie called "Roman Holiday" with Audrey Hepburn and Gregory Peck in which Hepburn plays a young princess of an obscure little country who is in Rome as she is making a multi-nation goodwill tour. She feels confined and frustrated by her royal life and runs away one night to explore the city. In the experiences during her exploration, she comes in contact with real people and once she goes back to her royal life, she better understands her responsibilities and what is expected of her in her role as a princess.

In the previous chapters, we have covered many areas that were designed for you to get an understanding of who you are in Christ and what rights you have as a member of the Royal Family of God. We cannot truly walk in our destiny, in the plans that God has designed for us, if we do not understand who we are in Christ and what our rights and promises are. Just as Hepburn's character in "Roman Holiday," she was playing a role as a princess that she did not understand; once the understanding came, she was determined to do her part and be what was expected of her in her role as a princess.

Do you have a better understanding of your position and rights as a princess of the Kingdom of God from the previous chapters? Explain in your own words some of the truths that you have learned so far.

_____

_____

_____

_____

_____

Now that you do have a better understanding of your position and rights as a royal, as a princess of God's Kingdom, now we must acknowledge that with this understanding comes responsibility.

As it says in Romans 12:10,

> *"Love each other with genuine affection,*
> *and take delight in honoring each other."*

As we learn to live out this life as a princess in the Royal Kingdom of God, one of the first things we are asked to do is to love each other with genuine affection. This comes straight from Jesus telling us what is expected of us under the New Covenant through Christ. In Matthew 22:37-40 (NKJV), when a Pharisee (who was trying to trip Him up, by the way) asked Jesus what the greatest commandment was, Jesus said to him,

> *"'You shall love the LORD your God with all your heart, with all your soul, and with all your mind.' This is the first and great commandment. And the second is like it: 'You shall love your neighbor as yourself. On these two commandments hang all the Law and the Prophets."*

The greatest commandment in the New Covenant is to love our God with all our heart, all our soul, and all our mind. But then the second is to love our neighbor as ourselves. Wow! Do you really understand what that is saying?

Love is used in so many different ways that we lose the true meaning behind that word. I can go to the furniture store and say "I love that lamp!" Or I can say, "I love summertime!" Unfortunately, the English language uses the same word "love" to express so many different types of love that the meaning can be quite underestimated.

When we look into the Greek word for love, we find four different types of love expressed by the same word "love." You must then use context clues to determine the meaning. The four types are eros, philia, storge, and agape, in no particular order.

Eros is defined as intimate love in the Modern Greek (erotas). It is the emotion shared when people are in love, the sensual passion that goes with being in love. In our society, even that has been skewed and manipulated so that you can be in and out of love in a blink of an eye. The original idea is to have a deep love for a person of the opposite sex and to make a commitment to one another.

Philia is an affectionate regard for another, such as brotherly love toward family, friends, and community. Storge is the love and affection specifically between parent and children, the natural love we have for our offspring. It can also be descriptive of a loyalty to county or a sports team.

And then there is agape. This is defined as the love of God for man and of man for God and is used to define the unconditional love that God has for his children.

And that is what we are talking about when we discuss loving our neighbor. There is an unconditional love our Heavenly Father has for His children and this love is in us from Him. We must learn to love unconditionally. That means to love when it is difficult, to be kind when it is not easy to be kind.

Matthew 5:43-47 says in the NKJV,

You have heard that it was said, 'You shall love your neighbor and hate your enemy.' [44] [a]But I say to you, love your enemies, bless those who curse you, do good to those who hate you, and pray for those who spitefully use you and persecute you, [45] that you may be sons of your Father in heaven; for He makes His sun rise on the evil and on the good, and sends rain on the just and on the unjust. [46] For if you love those who love you, what reward have you? Do not even the tax collectors do the same? [47] And if you greet your [b]brethren only, what do you do more than others? Do not even the [c]tax collectors do so?

Sometimes, the NKJV uses words and phrases in which the meaning is not clear, such as the reference to "tax collectors." These were considered some of the worst people in the day because most, if not all of them, cheated the people. They were dishonest and untrustworthy. So "even the tax collectors" love people who love them and are friendly to those who are friendly to them. That is not saying much about us Christians if we cannot do better than that.

The Message says it like this;

> *"You're familiar with the old written law, 'Love your friend,' and its unwritten companion, 'Hate your enemy.' I'm challenging that. I'm telling you to love your enemies. Let them bring out the best in you, not the worst. When someone gives you a hard time, respond with the energies of prayer, for then you are working out of your true selves, your God-created selves. This is what God does. He gives his best—the sun to warm and the rain to nourish—to everyone, regardless: the good and bad, the nice and nasty. If all you do is love the lovable, do you expect a bonus? Anybody can do that. If you simply say hello to those who greet you, do you expect a medal? Any run-of-the-mill sinner does that."*

If we are only loving people who are easy to love, then we as believers are not showing the world that we are any different or that there is a better way to live. We are called to love those who do not agree with us, who offend or persecute us. How do we do that? By showing kindness when it is not easy. By being patient when our nature is to be impatient and rude. By putting the needs and wants of others before our own.

It says in I Corinthians 13:1- 3 in the NIV,

> *"If I speak in the tongues of men or of angels, but do not have love, I am only a resounding gong or a clanging cymbal. If I have the gift of prophecy and can fathom all mysteries and all knowledge, and if I have a faith that can move mountains, but do not have love, I am nothing. If I give all I possess to the poor and give over my body to hardship that I may boast, but do not have love, I gain nothing."*

This is talking about the motives of the heart. If I am doing all this work to be important or to go through the motions of doing good but I don't actually love people, it is just wasted energy.

The Message makes it even clearer;

> *3-7 If I give everything I own to the poor and even go to the stake to be burned as a martyr, but I don't love, I've gotten nowhere. So, no matter what I say, what I believe, and what I do, I'm bankrupt without love."*

We may be doing good out of show, or we may be talking to people about God, but not showing them the true love of God. Or what if we are doing good but resenting the time it takes? What if it irritates us to give our money or have to interrupt something that we are doing to fulfill a need for someone? In those cases, we are just like a rusty gate. We are just making noise. Those kinds of acts do not last; they do not sustain life. They blow away with the wind.

I love this quote from Mother Teresa:

> *I am not sure exactly what heaven will be like, but I know that when we die and it comes time for God to judge us, he will not ask, 'How many good things have you done in your life?' rather he will ask, 'How much love did you put into what you did?*

How does this apply to being a princess in the Royal Kingdom of God? In our role as a believer, a member of this Kingdom, it is our responsibility to love people, to draw them into the Kingdom. We are to go beyond what the world expects and do what God expects. We are to love beyond what the world considers love to be. And we are to do it with joy and cheerfulness. Resenting the work that is being done is not God's love at all.

Let's look at some comments made in I John 4:7 (NKJV),

> *"Beloved, let us love one another,"*

Now here we are again being admonished to love one another, but notice

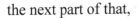

the next part of that,

> *"...for love is of God;"*

This kind of love in which we can love others comes from God. It is not a human love. It is a love, the agape love, that we can only demonstrate through the love of God that has been given to us from God.

Now notice this part,

> *"...and everyone who loves is born of God and knows God."*

This kind of love comes from someone who has been born of God, which is talking about being born of the spirit by receiving salvation which comes from the act of asking for forgiveness and asking Jesus to become one's Savior. Transformation begins that moment and then it is our responsibility to renew our mind in this love walk. The love of God has been put in our hearts at the moment of salvation when we become a family member of the Royal Kingdom of God.

Have you been transformed by receiving Jesus as your Savior? What should come next?

_____

_____

_____

_____

_____

Then it says in verse 8 of I John 4,

> *"He who does not love does not know God, for God is love."*

This is agape love; the type of love that loves regardless of the circumstances, regardless of what that person has done to me or what my day is like. When we can love when things don't go our way and when someone is rude or ugly to us, we have learned to love as God loves.

God shows us the ultimate agape love by sending His only Son down to earth to live among us and to take our place on the cross for our sins.

NIV says Verse 9 of I John 4 this way to make it clear,

> *"This is how God showed his love among us: He sent his one and only Son into the world that we might live through him. [10] This is love: not that we loved God, but that he loved us and sent his Son as an atoning sacrifice for our sins. [11] Dear friends, since God so loved us, we also ought to love one another. [12] No one has ever seen God; but if we love one another, God lives in us and his love is made complete in us."*

And then look what I find very significant in 1 Corinthians 13:11-12 (NLT),

> *"When I was a child, I spoke and thought and reasoned as a child. But when I grew up, I put away childish things. Now we see things imperfectly, like puzzling reflections in a mirror, but then we will see everything with perfect clarity. All that I know now is partial and incomplete, but then I will know everything completely, just as God now knows me completely."*

Now most of the time we are using this scripture when talking about growing into maturity in our walk with the Lord. We use it when discussing our behavior and maturity. It might be in a lesson about conflict resolution. But notice that this scripture is right in the middle of what is called the Love Chapter, 1 Corinthians 13, the all-in-all definition of love, the definitive explanation of what love is.

Parts of this chapter are used in weddings and such to reinforce the idea of love, God's love, and how we are to love others. And BAM! There is this scripture. Did it just get stuck in there to fill up space in this chapter? No, it was put in there to give more clarity concerning love. When we mature in God, we should be maturing in our love walk. And in doing so, we should be seeing ourselves with more compassion and mercy toward others.

As I mentioned earlier, transformation begins at the moment of the salvation. But then it is our responsibility as believers, as members of this Royal Kingdom, to pursue knowledge of our Heavenly Father and how to walk in the righteousness that He has asked us to do. We read the Bible. We study who God is, and we dissect Jesus' actions on earth to give us guidance in our new walk in the Lord.

We should be learning to walk in love as He did on this earth. This is what is bringing the maturity mentioned in verse 11-12. It is saying that we do not love in childish ways any longer but in a mature love that can only come from God who is in us. And as we grow in the Lord and in the knowledge of the character of Him, we grow in love and how to love others. We can only walk in this agape love with Him in us and with us every day.

I'll never forget the time that my mother and I were going to a large store to do some shopping. I got busy reading and texting something in my phone while we were walking across the parking lot. As I was walking across the pedestrian walkway to make it from the parking lot to the start, I slammed right into a sign. I looked around to see how many people saw me walk into that sign, and I saw my mother doubled over laughing. It was pretty funny and we laugh to this day about that moment of distraction.

I tell you this silly story about myself, though, to make the point that we can be so focused on what is going on in our lives and our problems that we will miss what is going on around us. Look up and open your eyes to what is going on around you. Be intentional in looking into people's faces, into their eyes and be aware of the suffering and anguish of the world we live in. You could be the one with the encouraging word that can put someone over in a time of need. You could be the one who shines a little light into a life of darkness. You may be the one who gives some love to a person who is starving for attention and affection.

What do you think childish love looks like? What are some signs that someone has grown in their love walk?

_____

_____

_____

_____

_____

I have heard people say that they were not sure that they could love as Christ did or that they do not have the capacity to love unconditionally. But that is actually opposite of what the Word says. Alas, do not lose hope, for it says that through the Holy Spirit who was given to us, God's love is poured into our hearts.

Romans 5:5 (NKJV) says,

> *"Now hope does not disappoint, because the love of God has been poured out in our hearts by the Holy Spirit who was given to us."*

We are talking God's love; the God kind of love is poured into your hearts. You have the capacity to love the way God loves. You have the potential to do acts of love towards others. If you are not pouring out this love toward others, don't blame your childhood, your background, or your personality. God overrides all of that by pouring His kind of love inside of you through the Holy Spirit which you received when you were born again. There is no excuse. It is expected of you as a child of the Living God to love as the Living God loves, unconditionally.

In the aforementioned movie, "Roman Holiday", the princess comes back from her adventures a different person. She has met real people and has experienced things that made her see other people for the first time and she realizes that she has some work to do in her position as princess of her kingdom. She basically grew up. She went from being treated like a child to expecting to be treated as the adult with responsibilities. It is the same with us. When we are first born again, we are a child craving the sincere milk of the Word.

The Bible says in 1 Peter 2:2 (NKJV),

> "...as newborn babes, desire the pure milk of the word, that you may grow thereby,"

As new Christians, we desire the milk or a simple message so that we may grow in our knowledge of Him. After some time, we are to begin desiring the meat of the Word. We start growing up and taking on responsibilities as Christians taking action and becoming doers of the Word. And now, with maturity, we are expected to put into action the Word that we have been feeding on.

Hebrews 5:14 says it this way in the NIV,

> "But solid food is for the mature, who by constant use have trained themselves to distinguish good from evil."

There are so many analogies that could be used here to get the point across. If I want to get better at playing basketball and want to make the team, then I need to spend time practicing the basics of basketball. The idea that practice makes perfect is actually incorrect. The right idea is perfect practice makes perfect. If I want to be able to show the coach that I am good, I need to be able to dribble correctly and fast. If I practice incorrectly by double dribbling, all the practice in the world is not going to make me better. So, learning the correct way to dribble and then practicing it over and over correctly will make me a good dribbler and I may make the team.

My husband has always said that Peyton Manning was a "student of the game"—the game of football. He is considered one of the best quarterbacks of football and much of his success came from his studies of the game, of his opponents, of his own team players. To become one of the best in his field, he had to take his studying seriously. He had to be focused on learning everything he could so that he would be successful.

The same can be said for living out our life of faith. If we don't spend time in the Word of God to find out what God says about certain things or to find out what He wants us to be like, then we are not going to be a better person or a better Christian.

When we talk about practicing the Word, we are saying to find out in the scripture what He expects of us and put it into practice in our everyday life. That is the practice of living as a child of the King, as a princess in the Kingdom of God. We must move on from the milk of the Word, the basics of being saved, and move on to the meatier things of the Word. We are to mature and grow in our knowledge of what He wants from us. If we are not growing in our knowledge of Him and His will, we are really just standing still.

What would you do to show love toward others? Name a few concrete ideas that someone could do to show love.

_____

_____

_____

_____

_____

2 Corinthians 13:14 (MSG) says,

"The amazing grace of the Master, Jesus Christ, the extravagant love of God, the intimate friendship of the Holy Spirit, be with all of you."

Let's live an extravagant love toward others. Not just at certain times of the year, but all year long and every day. As we step out in faith to love the unlovable or the one who offended us, or the one who we think doesn't deserve our love, God will use us in mighty ways to show His kind of love, the agape love that knows no bounds -- no sin that can't be forgiven and no offense that can't be rectified.

Mother Teresa said,

"Intense love does not measure. It just gives."

To give love means to act toward others in love. We are to do something to show our love. We can't just say we love; we must show this in action.

Your role as a princess in the Royal Kingdom of God is to love others; to show His love that has been shown to us. This love walk as a princess in the Kingdom is not to lord over others that we have something they don't have, but to share freely what has been given to us freely and to draw them to our Savior, Jesus Christ.

Once we have the understanding of what is expected, we must step up to do our part. This freedom we have received through the blood of Jesus opens up the door to serve one another in love.

1. What is the greatest commandment that Jesus gives us? How does that apply as we look into "The Role of a Princess"?

_____

_____

_____

_____

_____

2. What does it mean to have "an extravagant love of God"? Give examples of how we can put this into practice in our daily lives.

_____

_____

_____

_____

3. How do people know that we are His disciples and that we are diffe-

rent? Who in your life needs to see this love so that transformation can come and how can you make a difference?

_____

_____

_____

_____

4. What scripture in this chapter sparked your interest and why?

_____

_____

_____

_____

CHAPTER 9

The Duties of the Princess

Galatians 5:13 (NLT)

*"For you have been called to live in freedom, my brothers and sisters.
But don't use your freedom to satisfy your sinful nature.
Instead, use your freedom to serve one another in love."*

As we have been working through this book, I hope that you have grown in the knowledge that as a princess of the King, a child of the Living God and part of a royal priesthood, you have come to the definitive conclusion that you have worth and value in the eyes of the Lord and therefore, you have rights and benefits befitting a royal as part of the Royal Family of God. But not only do we have rights, privileges, and benefits, we also have responsibilities.

Because we have the Almighty God as our Heavenly Father, we have all that we need to live a life of joy and peace and abundance. In the previous chapter, we talked about the extravagant love that God has for us and that we have the ability to love others in the same manner because that love was poured into us. We have the love of God inside of us and with that love comes the responsibility of putting into practice that love in practical and meaningful ways.

We are to be known as disciples of Christ by our love, but to be recognized for that, we must put our hands and feet to work for Jesus. We must involve ourselves in the workings of the ministry to touch lives, to make a difference. We can sit in a pew every Sunday and be fed the Word of God and be encouraged by the Word that is given, but if we never put it into practice—if we don't become a doer of the Word as James 1:22 says in the NKJV—then we are just a storage container holding what we have but not pouring out God's love to others.

As we embark on this love walk, we also need to understand that there is always sacrifice for the things that are important. We should always have a part to play in the abundance in which we are rightfully living.

It says in Romans 12:1 (NIV),

Therefore, I urge you, brothers and sisters, in view of God's mercy, to offer your bodies as a living sacrifice, holy and pleasing to God— this is your true and proper worship.

As part of our worship to the God of mercy and grace, we are to sacrifice

—to *offer our bodies as a living sacrifice.* What does it mean to offer our bodies as a living sacrifice? When we receive Jesus into our hearts as our Savior, our spirit is immediately transformed because our sins are forgiven and we now have the spirit of God inside of us.

Then, as we grow in the Word and mature in the things of God, we renew our minds so that we can take our thoughts captive. We endeavor to think like God and to strive to live like Jesus. It is our bodies that have the hardest task of being changed so that we can live this life of holiness and righteousness that God expects of us.

In the years before we asked Jesus to be our Savior, we did what our mind and body wanted to do. We followed what the flesh wanted to do and did not know that it was leading to death – spiritual death. I would dare say that many are still living a life of mind and body decisions. If a new believer is not reminded or mentored to meditate on the Word of God or instructed to get in the Word to bring the mind and body in subjection to the spirit, then yes, he or she is still living a life of fleshly decisions.

It says in 1 Thessalonians 5:23 (NKJV),

> *"and may your whole spirit, soul, and body*
> *be preserved blameless at the coming of our Lord Jesus Christ."*

We must live a life of holiness to please our God and to keep our bodies as a living sacrifice. Making our body do the right thing in any given moment is difficult but doable if we will put the fleshly or worldly ideas away and begin to choose to do the godly thing. All three parts of us are to be found blameless. How do we do that? Let me break it down for you.

We are a three-part being. One part of our being is the spirit, which is transformed immediately upon receiving Jesus as Savior. When we are first born again, our spirit is weak in the things of God and our body has been doing what the flesh and the mind have wanted it to do. Our spirit, before being transformed by receiving Jesus as Savior, has sort of been lying dormant and has not had much to do with our decisions.

Another part of our being is the soul which is the mind, will, and emotions. This is the part of ourselves that makes the decisions of what we will be doing in our thought-life and in our bodies. Up until salvation, your mind, will, and emotions have ruled your thought processes, your pleasures, and your decisions and were influenced greatly by your body and what the body wanted.

The third part of our being is the body and it does what the soul tells it to do. Biologically speaking, your brain has control of your voluntary and involuntary actions. Involuntary would be stuff like heart rate, breathing, and things like that. The voluntary is what I mean when I say that the mind tells your body what to do. Some of what the mind tells the body to do are automatic, some are trained over time, and some are influenced by the things around it.

The body, or the flesh as it is often called in the Christian vernacular, is the part of our being that we must get control of. Paul says in 1 Corinthians 9:27 in the NKJV,

"But I discipline my body and bring it into subjection, ... "

Our physical body or our flesh will side with the stronger of the two—the spirit or the mind. If our spirit is stronger because we have been maturing and growing in the things of God, we can make our body do the right thing. If we let our mind, will, and emotions be stronger because we haven't been diligently putting the Word of God in to replace the old thinking, then we are still being ruled by the flesh, what the body wants and not what the spirit wants.

If our body is going to side with the stronger one, either the spirit or the mind, will, and emotions part – the soul, we must do all we can to build up our spirit in the things of God. To do that is to spend time with the Father in prayer and in His Word. Making your spirit stronger than your soul will bring victory in disciplining your body.

Just as we discipline our bodies in exercise or discipline our time management or discipline our spending habits, we should take this seriously and discipline our mind in spiritual things. This is our true and proper worship of God—to live a holy life pleasing to God and to accomplish that we must get our bodies in line with the Word of God.

Write in your own words how you would describe the phrase "your bodies as a living sacrifice."

_____

_____

_____

_____

_____

Another way to get our bodies to be a living sacrifice is to serve one another. As we continue in Romans 12, we will see that doing our part in the Kingdom by serving one another keeps the Kingdom working properly. The old man before salvation was a selfish man; that is the nature of one who does not know God.

We know this as we see our children grow from infancy. As they begin to walk and talk, they immediately demand "mine" when confronted with sharing a toy for the first time. As a responsible and caring parent, we take those teaching moments to begin the process of teaching our children to be caring toward others and to learn to share. Then as they grow, we as parents have to continue to deal with each incident of selfishness to teach them how to relate to others in play groups, in the classroom, as part of a family, and as a member of society. This is the natural process of teaching our children to not be selfish and to think of others.

This is the same concept as a child of God, but it takes it a little further because the world has its notions and ideology of what is acceptable, and that does not always line up with the Word of God. God expects more from His children. He expects us to go the extra mile in our love walk and in our representation of Him.

Once we become Christ followers, we are to put away our selfishness and try to be more like Jesus who came to earth to serve all of humanity. If Jesus was willing to give up all that He had in heaven so that we may live a joyous and fulfilled life, then it should be easy for us to sacrifice time and effort to serve one another in love. It is the new commandment under the new covenant through Jesus Christ.

We see in Romans 12:4-5 (NIV) that it says:

"For just as each of us has one body with many members, and these members do not all have the same function, so in Christ we, though many, form one body, and each member belongs to all the others."

We are all created by Him for a specific purpose. He has given us certain talents and gifts that He wishes us to use for the benefit of His Kingdom. He has of course given us the free will to use our gifts and talents for our occupation and hobbies, but He certainly wants us to serve the Kingdom of God by using the gifts and talents that He has given us.

Just as one body has many members, all the members have their different functions and then altogether, we belong as one so that the body functions properly. If we look at this like a machine, how would the machine work if not all the parts were working properly? What if one piece was missing in the machine; would it work as it is supposed to? No, of course not. There would be problems.

We have already established in a previous chapter that God created each of us in our mother's womb and that none of us was a mistake. God was purposeful in our creation and He had you and me in mind when He created each of us. No matter what our circumstances were in our childhood and the choices we made after our childhood, God was never taken by surprise. We must be confident that God had every intention for you to take your place in the Royal Family of God and to do your part in the building and spreading of His Kingdom.

Just as the farmer has a specific seed he plants in a certain location and then expects the fruit of his labor to coincide with what he planted, the Lord plants us in our mother's womb specifically so that we will fulfill the purpose and plan that God specifically established for us. Our job is to seek Him and be led by the Spirit so that we can follow that plan that God has designed for us. Then we can move forward one step at a time to see the fruition of His plan come to pass in our lives.

As I mentioned earlier, in the movie *Roman Holiday*, when Audrey Hepburn's character came to realize the seriousness of her position as a princess in the kingdom, she realized that she must sacrifice the whims and follies of a worldly life, and take up her responsibilities as a royal, to represent her family and her kingdom. We must see that for ourselves as well. We are princesses in the Kingdom of God and with that comes responsibilities to represent our Heavenly Father, to hold ourselves to a certain standard that would be pleasing to Him and that would draw people unto Him.

Now let's talk about what this looks like in our lives. Continuing in Romans 12, we see in Romans 12:6-8 (NLT):

> *"We have different gifts, according to the grace given to each of us. If your gift is prophesying, then prophesy in accordance with your faith; if it is serving, then serve; if it is teaching, then teach; if it is to encourage, then give encouragement; if it is giving, then give generously; if it is to lead, do it diligently; if it is to show mercy, do it cheerfully."*

Because we are part of a family, we must do our part in the Kingdom for it to function properly as a unit. We all have our part to do. Now what does that look like for you? What are you drawn or gifted to doing?

What are some of your gifts and talents? Name some things that you like to do? What makes you tick?

_____

_____

_____

_____

_____

As you ponder these things, think about how you could use what you listed above to help at your local church or community.

Now, a little bit of homework: Make a list of ministries in your church and around your community that could utilize your gifts, experience, and/or talents. Be creative and think outside of the box when making this list. Do an internet search of compassion ministries in your area. Ask your pastor about different ministries in the church or start a ministry for which you see a need.

_____   _____

_____   _____

_____   _____

_____   _____

_____   _____

_____   _____

Mother Teresa said once,

> *"Love cannot remain by itself – it has no meaning.*
> *Love has to be put into action, and that action is service."*

When people who are embroiled in some kind of stressful situation, especially one that is lasting a long time, come to me, I usually suggest that it is better to put themselves in a position of serving others for this takes their minds off of themselves and their problems. Love in action will refocus your mind and spirit so that you are not spending all your mental energy on yourself.

The Word says that Jesus was moved with compassion several times in His ministry. Compassion is the feeling that arises in one who is confronted with another's suffering. Compassion is the heartbeat of Jesus, and when we see suffering, we too should be moved with compassion. We are his hands and feet. We should be doing the work of the ministry. We are called—actually commanded—to do His works on this earth.

I Peter 4:10 says in the NLT:

> *"God has given each of you a gift from his great variety of spiritual gifts.*
> *Use them well to serve one another."*

As we have established throughout this book, God has created each of us for a purpose, and to step out in faith to put your hands to work in the ministry is the first step toward fulfilling your commission in the Kingdom of God. As a princess in the Kingdom of God, He has equipped you to serve in the Kingdom. We each have something that we can contribute to the workings of the ministry.

In Ephesians 4:12 it says "…for the equipping of the saints, for the work of the ministry." The church was never set up for the pastor to do everything in the church. He can't direct traffic in the parking lot, greet the people at the door, work in the nursery, usher people to their seats, take up the offering, and then get up on the platform to preach. We should not be expecting him to run every ministry, go to every meeting, plan and cook all the meals, and then have to time to pray and seek the Lord for the shepherding of the flock.

The pastors, teachers, evangelists, apostles, and prophets were put in place to teach, guide, and lead the laypeople to do the work of the ministry as it says in Ephesians 4:12. You are to find a place in your church to plant yourself and be productive for the Kingdom. Your list above should be a starting point if you are not already involved in your church. Pray about it and get plugged in. No more excuses!

Everyone, and I mean everyone, should be doing something in his/her church. If you are not working in your church right now, then now is the time to find your place. If you are already working in your church, then maybe it's time to stretch yourself and take the next step in leadership. God does not expect us to stay rooted without growth. He expects us to step out of our comfort zone because only then do we lean on Him and need Him. If you are doing something easy, then you should be looking for an opportunity to grow and step out of that comfort zone. What that means to you, I don't know. But what I do know is that you are equipped to do what God wants and needs you to do.

God may be speaking to you about doing something, but you may be unsure exactly what it is He expects. If you don't know what He wants you to do, just put your hands to work doing something. I've always said that it is easier to turn a moving car than a parked car. Waiting for your big break may never come if you are not already moving. Find a place to serve others in some way. Your local church needs you. Your community needs you. You have been put in this position as a princess in the Royal Kingdom of God for such a time as this and God is expecting big things from you.

1. What could it mean to offer your body as a living sacrifice?

_____

_____

_____

_____

_____

2. What does it mean to you to be a member of the body? What can we do to make sure the Kingdom is working at its best?

_____

_____

_____

_____

3. What have you been created for? How can you get involved to make a difference for God?

_____

_____

_____

_____

_____

4. What scripture do you want to apply to your life today? And why?

_____

_____

_____

_____

_____

CHAPTER 10

Be a Fearless Royal

Proverbs 31:25 NLT

*²⁵ She is clothed with strength and dignity,
and she laughs without fear of the future."*

When was the last time you laughed thinking about your future? The future of your marriage? The future of your children and their marriages? The future of your career and prosperity? You might think your situation is no laughing matter. But on the contrary, to be able to laugh without fear of the future means you have given it to the Lord, and you are confident that He will complete what He has started.

There is a certain freedom that you must be aware of to be able to laugh without fear of the future. Freedom to walk as a princess of the Kingdom of God comes with the responsibility of loving our God and loving others. Being able to live fearlessly and laughing without fear of the future is part of living out our lives as a fearless royal.

First of all, we must be fearless in Him. So far in this book, we have covered our position, role, and purpose as a member of the Kingdom of God. Knowing who He is and whose you are is the crux of it all. We have also covered the benefits of being part of this Kingdom and the rights and responsibilities that come with the honor of it. We also discussed the foundation on which our lives must be built and the fact that we must unload our luggage if we want to move forward in our lives.

If you have taken to heart the truths in this book and are applying them to your life, you are ready to now be fearless in Him, to be a fearless royal.

Job 10:10 says in the NLT,

"You guided my conception and formed me in the womb."

and

Psalm 139:15 also in the NLT,

"You watched me as I was being formed in utter seclusion, as I was woven together in the dark of the womb."

God was there from the beginning, even before you were conceived. He watched as you were being formed. There are no accidents. Some wonder if they were an accident. Some wonder if they really have a reason to be

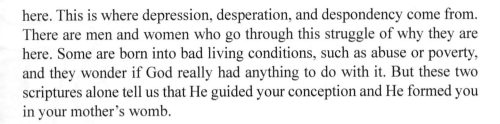

here. This is where depression, desperation, and despondency come from. There are men and women who go through this struggle of why they are here. Some are born into bad living conditions, such as abuse or poverty, and they wonder if God really had anything to do with it. But these two scriptures alone tell us that He guided your conception and He formed you in your mother's womb.

After ministering on this subject one Wednesday night at church, a lady came up to me to say that that comment alone gave her freedom. She had always been told that she was a mistake, but when she saw from scripture that God was there when she was being created, it opened her eyes to that truth and gave her a joy that she had not experienced before.

If we can understand and truly entrench this truth deep into our soul, mind, and heart, we could walk with our heads held high. We could walk through anything in life knowing that God wanted us here for a reason and that He is with us and for us. We could pull ourselves out of the junk that we have been dealt in life and walk with the confidence that we are children of the Living God and therefore heirs of all that He has.

Do you feel ready to be fearless in Him? What would it feel like to be able to laugh without fear of the future?

_____

_____

_____

_____

_____

If you are not living in this confidence, you need to write down these scriptures and put it around your house, and say it out loud whenever you see it to remind you —to imprint it deep inside of you. *"Faith comes by hearing, and hearing by the Word of God."* (Romans 10:17) It is evident in a person's life when they are walking in this knowledge.

Too many women believe their value comes from the man they are with, the children they have, or the career they've chosen. As Christian women, our value comes from who we are in Christ —a child of the Living God, an heir of God and joint-heir with Christ, a princess in the Kingdom of God, a member of the Royal Family of God. No matter what the world throws at us, if we truly understand and walk in this knowledge, we can stride and sometimes push through it with the confidence of a royal in the Kingdom of God.

Once you know who you are and you are confident in your inheritance, then you can be fearless in love. If we know and are confident in our God and our place and position with Him, we can walk boldly and fearlessly in love, not only toward Him but also toward others.

Now, this could be difficult for some. If you have been rejected, hurt, or mistreated, then it is difficult to turn around and become vulnerable in your love toward others. I have had people tell me that they don't have that kind of love in them. Some believe that they don't have the capacity to love as God loves. But God is not asking something of you that you cannot do. He has given us the ability to love through Him. When you take the risk to love someone, you can do this through the human part of you or you can do this through God by the Holy Spirit that is inside of you.

Romans 5:5 in the NKJV says,

"Now hope does not disappoint, because the love of God has been poured out in our hearts by the Holy Spirit who was given to us."

I noted this scripture in the previous chapter but it is significant here as well. This scripture tells us that He has poured out God's love (or God's kind of love) into our hearts. Now, that does not sound like a trickle or a sprinkle. The Word says "poured out." That sounds like He opened up our hearts and poured it right in. I am actually picturing a water pitcher with God's hand holding it and pouring His love into my heart.

We cannot say we don't have the capacity to love when it says right here that He poured it right into our hearts. I will say that it may not come as easily to some as it does to others, but that is where we put God's Word into action. It is our Christian responsibility to show others the God kind of love.

I John 4:12 in the Voice says,

"No one has ever seen God with human eyes; but if we love one another, God truly lives in us. Consequently, God's love has accomplished its mission among us."

The Living Bible says it this way:

"For though we have never yet seen God, when we love each other God lives in us, and his love within us grows ever stronger."

And in the New King James Version, it says,

"and His love has been perfected in us."

Remember, we've covered what "perfected" means. Perfected means to grow to maturity. Our love grows to maturity as we love others through the love of God that we have inside of us. This takes practice.

As we have discussed in a previous chapter, perfect practice makes perfect. We practice love on others. Think of it this way: Let's say you had a speech to give at a function and you are not very practiced in speech-giving. You would probably get someone to practice on or you would practice in front of a mirror. I've done both.

Practicing love can be the same way. You can't practice love in an incorrect way. If you show love to someone, you will be amazed at the response. You can start small but once you start, you will move swiftly to do more. Take my word for it, when you start putting love in action toward others and loving out loud, you will be amazed at how infectious it can become. Giving donations in the offering toward a ministry or activity is a wonderful way to bless others, but when you put your hands to work in the nitty-gritty of ministry, when you can see the faces of the people who are blessed by your actions, you will become obsessed with the doing of it.

Now, I admit that loving out loud can be risky, too. I am not naturally a huggy person and I've had to work on that. Not that hugging is "love" but hugging is a form of showing affection. Let me explain how this works for a person who is not a natural hugger.

It goes like this in the brain: "Ok, should I hug this person? If I move to hug, will he/she respond with warmth, or curiosity, or scorn? If I lean forward to hug, will that person move away or just stick a hand out for a shake?" These are the thoughts of the unnatural hugger. Now, for the natural hugger, this does not even go through their heads. They just go to hug, and you will hug them whether you want to or not.

So, for the person who has been hurt or mistreated, this is the same thing going through their head when it is time for them to decide to love or not. "If I show God's love toward this person, if I step out and show concern, love, or thoughtfulness toward this person, will I be accepted in warmth, or with curiosity or scorn? Will I be rejected or accepted? Will they laugh at me or will we stand there awkwardly?"

Because I have been working for the last few years with children who have had difficult childhoods, I have seen this time and again. The act of showing that they care is difficult for them because they feel that they are opening themselves up to be vulnerable. They have difficulty trusting and that includes trusting whether they will be accepted when they do show that they care. This is a risk that some are not willing to take and then their actions make people believe they do not care about other people, their education, or their future.

Is it easy or difficult for you to show love to others? Why do you think that?

_____

_____

_____

_____

_____

The Word says that the love of God is in us and the love that He pours into us gives us the ability to love like He does. We, out of love for Him, show love toward others. If we are confident that He loves us with our faults, our sin, and our blemishes, then we can turn around and love others unconditionally without fear of rejection. So, we must be fearless in love. We must take those risks and step out to show love toward others.

I John 3:23 says it this way in the Living Bible,

"And this is what God says we must do: Believe on the name of his Son Jesus Christ, and love one another."

We have two things to do with the love of God that is inside of us: believe in the name of Jesus and love one another. We must get past our past—our past hurts, our past mistakes, our past abuses, our past rejections, our past baggage. Because He makes us strong in our love because He loved us first and His love is inside of us.

To walk fearlessly in Him is to walk fearlessly in love, and now we can walk fearlessly in life. Understanding our position and place in Christ makes us fearless in love because we are loved first and unconditionally. If we are walking in love toward others fearlessly, and we know that we are loved by our Heavenly Father, this puts us in the mindset of doing life fearlessly. We are then able to step out and do what God wants us to do.

If we have been hurt in our past, it gives us the strength to move on and fulfill our destiny in God. If life has given us a curveball, we know that God was not surprised by this and He has a plan for us.

Jeremiah 29:11 says in The Message,

"I'll show up and take care of you as I promised and bring you back home. I know what I'm doing. I have it all planned out—plans to take care of you, not abandon you, plans to give you the future you hope for."

What does it mean to be a "Fearless Royal?" Let's look at Mary the Mother of Jesus as an example of living fearlessly. Here is a young woman, some say as young as 14, who is asked to do the unknown:

Luke 1:26-37 says,

Now in the sixth month the angel Gabriel was sent by God to a city of Galilee named Nazareth, ²⁷ to a virgin betrothed to a man whose name was Joseph, of the house of David. The virgin's name was Mary. ²⁸ And having come in, the angel said to her, "Rejoice, highly favored one, the Lord is with you; blessed are you among women!"
²⁹ But when she saw him, she was troubled at his saying, and considered what manner of greeting this was. ³⁰ Then the angel said to her, "Do not be afraid, Mary, for you have found favor with God. ³¹ And behold, you will conceive in your womb and bring forth a Son, and shall call His name JESUS. ³² He will be great, and will be called the Son of the Highest; and the Lord God will give Him the throne of His father David. ³³ And He will reign over the house of Jacob forever, and of His kingdom there will be no end."
³⁴ Then Mary said to the angel, "How can this be, since I do not know a man?"
³⁵ And the angel answered and said to her, "The Holy Spirit will come upon you, and the power of the Highest will overshadow you; therefore, also, that Holy One who is to be born will be called the Son of

God. [36] Now indeed, Elizabeth your relative has also conceived a son in her old age; and this is now the sixth month for her who was called barren. [37] For with God nothing will be impossible."

Then verse 38 (NKJV) says, *"Then Mary said, "Behold the maidservant of the Lord! Let it be to me according to your word."*

Was there any hesitation? Did she say, "Wait and let me pray about it or fast or consider the consequences"?

No, she knew her God and she walked in His love. She loved her Heavenly Father. It says in verse 30 that she had found favor with God. Well, to find favor with God is to please Him and to please Him is to have faith in Him and to walk in his commandments. She was willing to take the consequences of her actions because she chose to do what He asked of her. Put away by her betrothed, sent home and divorced, ostracized by the people, thrown out of her parents' home—any or all of the consequences could have happened to her and yet she was willing to take all this on to do His will. That is walking like a fearless royal.

Ruth is another example of living fearless. I'll give you a short synopsis of the beginning of the Book of Ruth, but be sure to read it for yourself as part of this study. It starts by telling us that a man along with his wife and two sons moved to Moab during a famine in Judah. They lived there for many years and the two sons married Moabite women.

After the man and his two sons die, these three women were left without anyone to take care of them. The older woman Naomi heard that Judah was doing well again and decided to go home. They began their journey when Naomi told her two daughters-in-law that they do not have to go with her. One of them, Orpah, decided to stay in her native country. But the other one, Ruth, chose to go with her mother-in-law. This is how Ruth responded to Naomi when Naomi encouraged her to go back to her home: Ruth 1:16 (NLT),

"Don't ask me to leave you and turn back. Wherever you go, I will go;

wherever you live, I will live. Your people will be my people, and your God will be my God. [17] Wherever you die, I will die, and there I will be buried. May the LORD punish me severely if I allow anything but death to separate us!"

She chose to stay with Naomi and to love Naomi's God. She loved Naomi and obviously Naomi's love for her drew her to God as well. This also tells us what a great influencer Naomi must have been for Ruth to love her enough to leave her native home and family to go with Naomi to a strange country. Going with Naomi was a huge step for Ruth for she chose to go to an unknown land, without a guaranteed place to live or a husband to take care of her. That is living fearless in life because of her love for Naomi and for Naomi's God.

Do you see yourself as a Mary or a Ruth living fearlessly? Explain.

_____

_____

_____

_____

_____

Sometimes we have to step out and do the unknown because God has spoken to us. How many of us put off dreams because we don't know exactly how it is going to work out? How many of us have to have it all worked out before we step out? I know that I have been working on this book for a long time before I decided that I had to step out in faith and finish it. God has spoken several times to me to get this finished for He had a message to get out there and if I didn't do it, He would find someone else to do it.

Proverbs 31:25 in the New Living Translation
²⁵ She is clothed with strength and dignity,
and she laughs without fear of the future. "

I could not figure out how I was going to get this published without spending a fortune and working a full-time job. I was trying to see too far in advance and it was holding me back from fulfilling this dream. I was trying to work it out in my own strength and in my own plan. So, as I am writing this book, it is ministering to me as well. This topic is one that I have worked through as well. I had to laugh without fear of the future of this book, because I know that this is His will.

Do some of us have unsure futures? Maybe we don't know what is going to happen next? Do we have to know several steps in the future? Do we have to know the end result? How many of us wonder where we will be in a few years? Look to God and His love for us. We have looked at Jeremiah 29:11 in the Message. Now let's look again at it in NKJV,

"For I know the plans I have for you," declares the Lord, "plans to prosper you and not to harm you, plans to give you hope and a future."

To be a fearless royal, we must first know who our God is and understand our position with Him—that we are His heirs. We are Kingdom kids. We are His children and therefore we have rights to all that is His.
We must then understand that the unconditional love from God is what gives us the confidence to love others unconditionally and fearlessly.
Then, if we spend time with Him, knowing that we have a right to stand before Him, loved and cherished, we can hear His voice and we can step out and do what He has called us to do. Do you think you've missed your opportunity? Not a chance!
Because look what He says in Psalms 138:8 (NKJV),

"The LORD will perfect that which concerns me; "

This is the scripture that I have been standing on recently. Whatever concerns me, He will perfect it or bring it to maturity and completion. He knows your concerns. He knows your dreams and aspirations. He wants what is best for His children. He wants what is best for you. You are a princess in the Royal Kingdom of God.

Whatever has happened in your life, God was not surprised or deterred. He knows and has prepared you for your calling and purpose. God sent His only begotten Son that we may live abundantly and have a purpose. He sent Him for us and here in Isaiah 61:1-3 (NIV), He tells us specifically why He came.

"The Spirit of the Sovereign LORD is on me,
because the LORD has anointed me
to proclaim good news to the poor.
He has sent me to bind up the brokenhearted,
to proclaim freedom for the captives
and release from darkness for the prisoners,
2 to proclaim the year of the LORD's favor
and the day of vengeance of our God,
to comfort all who mourn,
3 and provide for those who grieve in Zion—
to bestow on them a crown of beauty
instead of ashes,
the oil of joy
instead mourning,
and a garment of praise
instead of a spirit of despair.
They will be called oaks of righteousness,
a planting of the LORD
for the display of his splendor."

Do you find yourself in there? Are you grieving for a person or a forgotten dream? Are you in a darkness that you cannot seem to get yourself out of? Do you feel a prisoner of some sort or in despair?

Maybe it is not that severe. Maybe you just feel stuck and that you don't feel like you have anything to offer the Kingdom of God. I've met plenty of women who don't have any idea what they are supposed to be doing

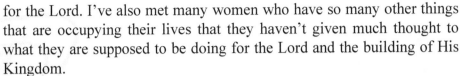

for the Lord. I've also met many women who have so many other things that are occupying their lives that they haven't given much thought to what they are supposed to be doing for the Lord and the building of His Kingdom.

I had a young mom tell me once that she did not feel that she had anything to offer because she was just an at-home mom. I encouraged her to use her gifts and talents for the Lord in whatever capacity she felt comfortable, and eventually she became very involved in her church's women's ministries.

My prayer is that this book has put tools in your hands to help you find your purpose and inspiration to do God's will in your life. We all have a purpose in this Kingdom that we are born into. We all have a reason for being here on this earth and for being a part of the Body of Christ.

To be a fearless royal is to understand who we are in Christ, knowing our benefits, and putting our hands and hearts to work in the Kingdom of God. Let's end with this – John 14:12 (NKJV):

"Most assuredly, I say to you, he who believes in Me, the works that I do he will do also; and greater works than these he will do, because I go to My Father."

Who is the "he" in this scripture? It can be confusing, but it is saying "the person who believes in Jesus" will do the works of Jesus and will even do greater works than Jesus did. Is that possible? All things are possible to those who believe. We are going to stand on the Word of God, and it says that we will do greater works. That is not man's opinion, but a truth from the scriptures—the truth.

Be a pursuer of dreams. Rediscover that dream that He put in your heart and pursue it. Take the necessary steps in the Lord to accomplish what He has inspired you to do.

Be a kingdom builder. You are a princess in the Royal Kingdom of God and you have certain responsibilities to fulfill. Find your place in this Kingdom and a part of this movement of drawing people to Him.

Be an overcomer. He has given you all that you need to handle your past and put it where it does not haunt or bother you ever again – in His hands.

Be a fearless royal. He has given you a purpose and the tools to fulfill that

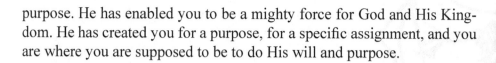

purpose. He has enabled you to be a mighty force for God and His Kingdom. He has created you for a purpose, for a specific assignment, and you are where you are supposed to be to do His will and purpose.

Now let's get down to work and go about our Father's business.

1. How does it make you feel when you read Psalm 139:15, "You watched me as I was being formed in utter seclusion, as I was woven together in the dark of the womb"?

_____

_____

_____

_____

_____

2. What are some ways that you can be "fearless in love" toward others? Do you find it difficult to show love? If so, why do you think that?

_____

_____

_____

_____

_____

3. What does living fearlessly look like to you? What would it take for you to step out in faith?

_____

_____

_____

_____

_____

4. What scripture(s) stood out to you from this chapter and why?

_____

_____

_____

_____

_____

CONCLUSION

My Prayer for You

LORD, I pray that the ladies who have read this book were touched by this message that I believe came from You. We are your children, your princesses, and I pray that each one of us understands how precious we are in your sight. I pray that each lady learned important truths that will help them to be overcomers, pursuers of dreams, and Kingdom builders.

LORD, I also pray that each lady will hear your voice and follow the path that you have designed for her. Help her to fulfill the calling and purpose that you have given her. Create in her the boldness to step out in faith and take the next step to influence others around her in her world, in her circumstances.

LORD, you know my story of how long it took me to finish this book, and I pray that this book can be a catalyst to propel these ladies to do Your will in their lives. Thank you, Lord, for being a big God and a holy God. Thank you that you are a God of second and third and fourth chances. You never give up on us. You are long-suffering and full of grace and mercy. Give us the fortitude, the strength, and the confidence to be the princesses that you want us to be.

In Jesus' name, Amen.

I have thoroughly enjoyed putting this book together to encourage and empower you to go after what God has designed for your life. He is a big God and holy God and He loves you unconditionally. The Holy Spirit will guide you in your step of faith as you envision your life with His divine purpose in the forefront, and while Jesus holds you hand through it all, your Heavenly Father is holding you in His hands.

Visit my blog:
http://www.preciouspromises124.com/

Check us out at:
www.trinityalgood.com

And if you are ever in the Cookeville/Algood, TN area, please visit us at:

TRINITYalgood
205 W. Wall Street
Algood, Tennessee 38506